WHEN WORK TAKES CONTROL

WHEN WORK TAKES CONTROL

The Psychology and Effects of Work Addiction

Pernille Rasmussen

KARNAC

First published as *Når arbejdet tager magten* in 2005 by
Hans Reitzels Publishers
Copenhagen

First published in English in 2008 by
Karnac Books Ltd
118 Finchley Road, London NW3 5HT

Translated by Susie Daugaard Hansen

British Library Cataloguing in Publication Data

A C.I.P. for this book is available from the British Library

ISBN: 978 1 85575 593 2

The WART test (p. 43) has been reproduced by permission of New York
University Press.

Edited, designed and produced by The Studio Publishing Services Ltd
www.publishingservicesuk.co.uk
e-mail: studio@publishingservicesuk.co.uk

www.karnacbooks.com

CONTENTS

ACKNOWLEDGEMENTS

I would like to thank Associate Professor Thomas Nielsen from the University of Aarhus, for discussions and guidance in relation to the dissertation which was the starting point of this book, and Editor Henriette Thiesen from Hans Reitzels Publishers, for her breadth of view, her thoroughness, and for always taking time out to be my sparring partner. Our informal talks and the good atmosphere helped me in my work with the book.

I am grateful to the many people who unreservedly told me their stories about how work had controlled their lives or the lives of their loved ones, as well as everyone who has spontaneously told me about their job situations, work habits, and lives in general, when they heard that I was working on the subject.

Thanks are also due to occupational health psychologist Einar Baldursson for an informative and inspiring interview, and psychologists Florence McLean, Camilla Kjærsgaard, Simi Voss, and Tine Grynnerup for their intellectual sparring with me or reading of passages of the book.

New York University Press gave permission to use the test (WART) on pp. 43, for which I thank them.

Finally, my grateful thanks to Susie Daugaard Hansen for translating the manuscript into English.

Pernille Rasmussen is a graduate in psychology and has worked for several years as an occupational psychologist for both the public sector and for private companies. She is influencing the debate about workaholism, stress, and work–life balance in Denmark, and is a member of several panels of experts. Pernille Rasmussen teaches and inspires people in her workshops and lectures, and she also coaches managers and individuals. She has written several articles for newspapers and magazines. For more information please visit the website www.growpeople.dk.

PREFACE

A couple of years ago, I started wondering why work is mentally such a large part of many people's lives. In the West, we are very committed to our jobs and, to a large extent, we identify ourselves by our work titles. We are generally very focused on being highly productive, and this means that a large number of people are constantly "doing something". Many people push themselves too hard with work, thus neglecting relaxation, hobbies, and other leisure activities, such as spending time with their families and friends. I, myself, find that I have a need to be productive and to utilize my time to the fullest. This way of life often leads to stress. What is it that drives us? Are we trying to escape from uncomfortable emotions and thoughts by working too much? Or do we think that our jobs are so interesting that we perceive them as hobbies? Maybe we are just ambitious and want to show the world how good we are at our jobs?

I set out to explore why some people work excessively and what some of the consequences are of doing so. What do these people have in common? I went through the research results and the literature on the subject and on the basis of this I wrote this book. While working on the book, I have spoken to many people about their personal experiences of a life dominated by work. Others have shared their experiences of being related to a workaholic. In addition, business managers have shared their views on how we avoid work taking over our lives.

The purpose of this book is to explain, first, what happens when we become too involved in our work, and, second, how we avoid being controlled by our work and how we prevent family members, friends, colleagues, or employees from being so. In addition, I hope the book will help bring about a debate about our work habits and initiate thought and discussion about our values and how much space work should be allowed to take up in our lives.

The book is addressed to everyone who deals with the psychological working environment, among them business managers and counsellors who treat people with work-related problems. In addition, anyone who wishes to establish a better balance between their work life and private life would benefit from reading the book.

Pernille Rasmussen
May 2008

CHAPTER ONE

Introduction

Through the ages, work has been the basis of the survival of the human race, and it has been an important and necessary part of our lives. Today—as opposed to former times—it is no longer necessary that we work all day long. Still, we live in a time when work, both mentally and in terms of time consumption, takes up a lot of space in many people's lives. Most jobs are limited to a certain number of hours per week. In France, it is thirty-five hours per week, and in Denmark the working week is thirty-seven hours. But, in spite of this, a large number of Europeans experience that this limit is overstepped time and time again, so that work intrudes on their spare time. Many people know the feeling of slowly being controlled by their job to the point that it becomes the very essence of their life. A large number of us are actually addicted to our jobs to a certain degree. This addiction is not financial, but rather psychological or even physical.

Most of us have tried working overtime for a certain period of time. Sometimes a large number of tasks may find their way to our desk, a deadline has to be kept, or a certain project may take up a great deal of time. Several different situations may make it impossible for us to stay within the number of hours we are supposed to work each week. In situations like these we may choose to work both evenings and weekends. To contribute something out of the ordinary from time to time at work does not mean that you are addicted to your work—if it is only for a limited period of time. A person addicted to his or her job, however, will often claim that the extra workload *is* limited to a certain period. "It's a bit busy at the moment, but it will soon be better." Comments like these will have become familiar to family members, who are told how things will eventually change and that they will soon spend more time together. Often the family members wait in vain. The extra workload is seldom limited to a specific period. New important assignments keep turning up, which the workaholic thinks that he or she needs to deal with. This situation follows a pattern (Fassel, 1992). Which factors are involved when we work too much? What do we gain by it?

To the workaholic, his or her job is very important, and it occupies a great deal of the person's time. The partner, the children, leisure activities, and friends are often put aside. The workaholic finds it difficult to take time off work because of a guilty conscience or the restlessness that creeps up on him or her when he or she is not at work. When workaholics eventually do take some time off and spend time with family and friends, they will find it difficult to relax and to be present in the moment. The workaholics will often be absentminded because their thoughts are on the job (Robinson & Chase, 2001). The workaholics are driven by deep-seated psychological needs rather than external needs. In other words, the workaholics are not working to be able to afford a nice present for their partner, or because the children need new clothes—even though many of them claim that they work too much for the sake of the family. The driving force behind the work addiction is the deep-set satisfaction that the work process brings to the workaholic (Robinson, 1998a). One could say that the addiction to work is centred on the adrenalin kick and the recognition from one's colleagues that often follow when one performs a quantitatively and qualitatively great work effort.

Many people have jobs in which they are not themselves able to control the workload; these kinds of jobs demand a long working week and a great deal of commitment. One could claim, based on this, that it is therefore the workplace and the type of job you have that decides if you will become addicted to your job. Research, however, implies that the workaholics are inclined to apply for jobs that demand an extra effort; in doing so, they choose to live lives dominated by their jobs. Individuals who are not likely to become addicted to work will often be unable to thrive within a company culture that requires him or her to "marry" the job. If you are predisposed to develop a work addiction, the environment, including your family and the workplace, will be a deciding factor in determining if this happens. The question is, then, how do we know if our work is taking control of our life? What are the signs, and what do you do if work has taken control of your life, or the life of a friend, a colleague, or a partner?

Workaholics can be found, to a certain degree, within most jobs, but most of them are found within the so-called knowledge-intensive professions (Rasmussen, 2004a,b). Within these professions, working hours are often not fixed, and it is the actual tasks rather than the clock that dictate when it is time to go home. This is in sharp contrast to unskilled labour and workmen whose work hours are often more structured and, to a much larger degree, adhered to. Some workmen, however, often work overtime, and it is possible to find workaholics within this sector. Thus, workaholics can be workmen (skilled or unskilled), kindergarten teachers, chefs, engineers, journalists, self-employed people, and so on.

It is a privilege to have a job that you find exciting and that you look forward to going to every morning. It may also bring you a great deal of satisfaction to work with something that you are really passionate about. It should, therefore, be seen as neither wrong nor dangerous to be committed to, and willing to go the extra mile for, one's workplace. What we should pay attention to, however, is whenever our job begins to control us so that we no longer have time to do anything but work. When we can no longer achieve balance in our life, it is time to come to a halt and to reassess the situation.

Wayne Oates presented the term "workaholism" thirty years ago, and his book, *Confessions of a Workaholic*, was the first to touch upon the subject. In the book, Oates describes how workaholics behave compulsively when it comes to work, just like alcoholics do in regard to alcohol (Oates, 1971). Today, three decades later, experts in the field still do not agree on how the phenomenon should be defined and understood. A few of them see workaholism as something positive. They claim that people who work excessively are merely conscientious, hardworking, and have more energy than other people. Therefore, they see these people as an asset to any company that employs them (Korn, Pratt, & Lambrou, 1987; Machlowitz, 1980). Other experts refrain from taking a position on the question of whether workaholism is a positive phenomenon or not, but instead concentrate on other areas of the phenomenon such as personality (Scott, Moore, & Miceli, 1997). In the course of this book, workaholism will be understood in the way shared by the majority of experts in the field. Most experts, including the most prominent, perceive workaholism as an addiction comparable to other forms of addiction. They point to the fact that there are varying degrees of addiction and describe a severe addiction to work as an affliction (Burke, 2000; Fassel, 1992; Killinger, 1991; Robinson, 1998a). Work addiction, in this book, will be defined as *an obsessive need to work. The workaholic will often work more hours than the average population; most other activities such as spending time with family and friends as well as leisure activities are not given a high priority.*

In the USA, they are now recognizing work addiction as a phenomenon. The amount of American research in the field, however, is limited, despite the fact that in many areas the USA is the leading nation with regard to psychological research. The limited research in the USA, as well as in the rest of the world, may be due to the fact that the field is a relatively new one, and that experts do not agree on how the field should be defined and understood.

In Denmark, there is a lot of talk about stress and burn-out, and for good reason, as one in four Danes experience work-related stress (Netterstrøm, 2002). In several cases, the stress is caused by a form of work addiction, and it is therefore important that we pay attention to this phenomenon. I hope that this book will help to bring work addiction and its consequences into focus. When we do not acknowledge work addiction in Denmark, it is probably because there has not been enough focus on the subject. In order to change, this and to make work addiction a subject discussed in the workplaces and by politicians, it is vital that we research the field. In this way, data will support the claim that we are facing a social challenge.

At the moment there are no Danish studies of the phenomenon. This may be due to the fact that this type of addiction is the only one that is rewarded by society and is associated with a certain degree of prestige. This book is based mainly on research from the USA. My experience is that we Danes copy the American way of life to a large extent, and we may therefore benefit from the knowledge collected in America. The existing knowledge in Denmark, in relation to people's over-involvement in their work, has so far come from experts who express their concern about the rising number of stress cases caused by people working too much over long periods of time (Baldursson, 2004). In Denmark, there is no specific treatment for severe cases of workaholism, such as we find in other countries. In the USA, Canada, France, and the UK there are, furthermore, self-help groups called "Workaholics Anonymous", which work in the same way as Alcoholics Anonymous, and are free of charge (Robinson, 1998a).

Due to the limited amount of research in the field, there are still many unanswered questions when it comes to work addiction. For example, there are, as yet, no studies that determine the number of workaholics—either in Europe or in the USA. For this same reason, it is also impossible to say anything on the gender division among workaholics.

It is important to point out that in this book I understand work addiction as something to do with one's main occupation. This means that the addiction is only related to the work and one's commitment to it. It is therefore not possible to be addicted to one's stamp-collection, golf-playing, or other hobbies. Work, however, should not be understood as merely paid work, but as *the activity that occupies the main part of an individual's waking hours*. Defined in this way, work includes schoolwork, studies, housework, as well as voluntary work, as long as it is the main occupation of the individual.

In the course of the book I will use interviews and statements from people who have experienced that work took control. Names, ages, and other characteristics have (at the request of the individual) been changed, allowing the interviewee to remain anonymous. The case examples are included in order to describe some of the different characteristics and situations that define work addiction, as well as to illustrate the different theories and themes within the field. The interviews include both men and women, as it is possible for both sexes to be controlled by their work. For linguistic purposes, the workaholic is, in most cases, termed "he", but in all cases the workaholic could just as easily have been a woman.

CHAPTER TWO

Work: curse or blessing?

"Americans generally spend so much time on things that are urgent that they have none left to spend on those that are important"

(Henry Ward Beecher, quoted in Robinson, 1998a, p. 233)

D o we work to live or do we live to work—this is a relevant question to ask today, when a large number of people spend considerable amounts of their time at work. In contrast to earlier times, when work was considered a necessary evil, work today seems to be what many people live for. What are the reasons for this development? There are, of course, many different reasons for the zeal that many people show when it comes to work today. Some of the explanations will be highly individual and depend entirely on the person you ask. In this chapter, we look at the significance of religion when it comes to our attitudes towards work. In addition, I examine how much the Danes work and go through some of the circumstances that lead people to push themselves, on a daily basis, by working excessively hard.

Religion and attitudes towards work

Going back to ancient Greece and the Roman Empire, before the birth of Christ, work was an object of contempt (Lindhardt & Urhskov, 1997). If you were working it meant that you were not free, and slaves were kept for doing whatever work needed to be done. Freedom was defined as "being free from work". A person forced to work was accordingly "un-free" and was not considered a member of society. The Greek philosophers Plato and Aristotle thought that Man should devote himself to such activities as philosophy, art, and politics. According to Aristotle, the contemplative life, consisting of reflection and the search for truth, was held in the utmost regard. Many different cultures around the world still perceive work as a low status activity and, accordingly, see it as a female occupation.

In our society, the perception of work has changed throughout history. The attitudes we hold about work today have their roots in Christianity. Christian values are the foundation on which our society and culture are built, and, accordingly, they also influence our perception of work. These Christian values have, in other words, influenced our work morals. In the Old Testament, as in the ancient world, work was seen as something performed by low-status members of society. In Paradise, man lived a free and carefree existence, but the punishment for Sin was work. When God drove Adam and Eve out of the Garden of Eden, he cursed the earth, saying, "Cursed is the ground because of you; in pain you shall eat of it all the days of your life; thorns and thistles it shall bring forth for you; and you shall eat the plants of the field. By the sweat of your face you shall eat bread . . ." (Genesis 3: 17–19). From that moment on, work became a curse, a necessary evil that man had to live with. Work, according to the Bible, was treated with contempt, but later on it was greatly valued. One of the reasons why work was eventually perceived as positive was that in the beginning Christianity was a working-class religion, which had many followers among the poor and slaves. These people's lives consisted of nothing but work, and the Church therefore had to represent work in its teachings as something worth doing. A parallel was formed to the hard work performed by God when He created the world.

The sixteenth century saw the rise of Puritanism in Northern Europe (Lindhardt & Urhskov, 1997). According to the Puritans, hard physical as well as spiritual labour was the only way to salvation. All sensual and sexual pleasures had to be avoided, as they were the works of the devil. Work could help people to live controlled and ascetic lives. This pleased God. The best way to stay on the right path was to work. During the same period, Martin Luther's thoughts had a profound impact on thousands of people and their attitudes towards both religion and work. Even today, the attitude towards work in Germany and Scandinavia can be traced back to the Lutheran reformation. Luther saw work as a concrete action showing that you love your neighbour (*ibid.*). By working, you show that you live by the commandment of loving one's neighbour. According to Luther, a good Christian is defined by how much he or she works. The Lutheran reformation led to a glorification of work, and it became a religious calling. We were now called to work by God. In German, work is *Beruf*, which actually means calling. Luther was also on his guard against idleness, which had to be fought because being idle could lead to sinful desires. The old saying, "Idleness is the root of all evil", has its origin in religion and can be traced back to the rules followed by monks. The monks were required to occupy any leisure time between prayers with work, so as to avoid sinful thoughts. The saying is still used today, thereby indirectly helping to maintain a perception of work several centuries old.

The German economist and sociologist Max Weber has united work, morals, and religion in the term: "the protestant work ethic" (Weber, 1995). He coined the phrase in an attempt to explain why some people are willing to work more than is necessary for them to survive. The Protestant way of thinking has shaped cultures and societies in Europe and the USA, and Weber consequently felt that there had to be a connection between this way of thinking and our attitudes towards work.

Activity and efficiency are central to the Protestant work ethic. The attitude towards time is essential. "Wasting time" is a great sin. A person who is working is not sinning. A person who is not working is at risk of being consumed by sinful desires, mainly of a sexual nature. Besides, work in itself is a divine goal. This is why the rich cannot lie back and live off their money. They should not relax, but strive to administer their money in the best possible way as well as try to make more. These attitudes create what Weber terms "the spirit of capitalism" (ibid.). The Protestant work ethic includes an admiration and respect for hard work and the belief that a great effort is worth while because it leads to success. This is the reason why several experts describe work addiction as "the addiction others admire" (Robinson, 1998a), as well as "the most respected and socially accepted addiction" (Killinger, 1991). Weber points to the fact that work no longer has a purpose but has become a purpose in itself. We have to work because we need to work. This means that work no longer has any limits, it has become an ongoing process which never ends.

Today, work has almost become a sacred duty in the Western world. Many people do practically nothing but work. They are literally working themselves to death. The perceptions from former times of work being both a curse and later on a blessing, are both characteristics of our perception of work today. It is a curse because the pace is fast and the demands on our commitment and our performance are high. But it is also a blessing because the physical framework has improved, and because many jobs afford the employee opportunities of both professional and personal development. Work is very important to us, and, as a consequence, we feel sorry for the unemployed. They are standing somewhere outside the community, and are seen as having nothing to live for. In ancient times it was the workers who were looked down on and who were standing on the outskirts of the community. Today, it is the other way round, mainly because we define ourselves and each other by our jobs. What is most valued in modern society, and what is also the most important tool for the integration of people into society, is professional work. This is a paradox (Beck, 2002).

As we have seen, Christianity has played an important role in determining how we relate to work. Our religion has been a contributing factor in a development that has led to work today taking up such large amounts of most people's time and lives. We now take a closer look at how many hours Danes spend working, then we look at the qualitative aspects that may help to explain why our jobs have become so important to us.

How much do Danes work?

A study carried out in 2000 by the Danish National Institute of Occupational Health of self-employed people and employees, showed that one in seven has a long working week. This means that they are working a minimum of forty-eight hours per week. The people who work this much are mostly self-employed, registered child-minders, male academics, and managers. The majority of people working long weeks are between thirty and fifty-nine years old; 22% are male and 8% are female. There are also large differences in gender when it comes to how much a person works each day. Three times as many men as women have a long workday (minimum ten hours), and three times as many women as men have part-time jobs. It is the men, then, who do the most paid work (Arbejdsmiljøinstituttet, 2000). Recent research shows that considerable health risks are connected with long working hours, for example, the risk of heart disease is considerably increased (Netterstrøm, Laursen, & Paludan, 1996). The numbers above relate only to paid work. Chores around the house, which are necessary for a family to function, have not been included. Even though men have started doing more chores around the house than was the case earlier, it is still the women who do the most work in this particular area. Women daily spend three and a half hours on housework—a whole hour more than the men (Bonke, 2003).

It turns out that a large group of Danes actually want to work more. A study from 1999, carried out by Sonar (Institute for Market and Opinion Polls) showed that one in four (25%) were willing to work more (and thereby make more money). Longer work hours and more money were more attractive to men than to women. In particular, the 18–49-year-olds were willing to work more (Sonar & Jyllands-Posten, 1999).

Many people take the opportunity of working from home, and the number of actual "home offices" have risen dramatically over the past couple of years. About one in five Danish employees works from home, either full-time or part-time (Hundevadt, 2003). The actual number may be even higher, as many people read specialist literature and e-mails or speak on the phone with colleagues about work in the evenings when they are at home. This all counts as work, but may not be included in the person's account of his or her work hours.

Many people see being able to work from home as an advantage, because this allows them a large degree of flexibility in relation to their family. One of the downsides, however, is that people tend to work more than is necessary when they work from home. The home office makes us able to work all hours of the day, and this is dangerous for those who have difficulties with limiting their work hours. New technology has made it possible for us to work at home as well as almost anywhere else. Laptops and mobile phones enable us to communicate and work whether we are on a beach in the Caribbean or on the train to Manchester. We are able to bring our work with us wherever we go, and to be constantly online and available. We are only "off" when we choose to turn of all devices.

Our jobs have invaded our private sphere and are creeping unhindered into our nights and holidays. Leisure time and work are now merging for thousands of people. It is up to each individual person to say "stop!", and put a limit on his or her work hours. This is difficult for most people, as there are no correct answers to the problem and no one with any experience in the field, whom we can ask for guidance. To limit one's work hours and to remember to take time off is a completely new discipline that is difficult to master. The people who are slow to catch on may develop an addiction to work, suffer from stress, or simply burn out.

It is debatable whether we actually work more or less than in former times. Within the past 100 years, the formal work hours have been reduced. In 1919, the Danish labour movement succeeded in getting the workday reduced to the point that no person should work for more than eight hours a day (Bendtsen, 1985). This reduction represented great progress, meaning that employees now had spare time to spend as they pleased. Since then, the eight hours a day limit has been changed, and today it is acceptable if the workday exceeds the eight hour limit. Today, it is the length of the working *week* rather than the *day* which is in focus. Looking at this development historically, the formal working week in Denmark has never been shorter than it is now (*ibid.*).

Denmark is actually one of the countries among the OECD countries that has the shortest work hours. Only the Netherlands, Sweden, and Norway have shorter work hours. In spite of this, many Danes work more and more (Bonke, 2003). For a large number of people the workday never really ends. This is caused, among other things, by optimization and an increasingly fast pace, which again is related to the technological developments of our day. Even though the work hours has officially been reduced, and work has now become less of a physical burden, many people still feel stressed and feel that great demands are put on them in the workplace.

Pressed for time

With the entry of the computer into almost all forms of workplaces, technology has been a deciding factor in increasing the work pace. Work processes, as well as the way we do things, are becoming increasingly efficient, and we are always trying to optimize further. This is because time is money. This statement has been generally accepted for several years now. The faster you are, the more money you will make—or, put more precisely, the more money the company you work for will make. With globalization and the increasing competition between companies to be the best and the cheapest, it has become necessary to be more and more efficient. An increasing number of companies are even outsourcing certain jobs. This means that jobs are moved abroad, to countries where they can be done for lower wages. In times of recession, cutbacks and employee dismissals are on the menu. The constant demands for efficiency and the increasing pace force the individual employee to contribute more.

Studies have shown that the work pace has increased and that work has become more intense within the past twelve years (Netterstrøm, 2002). If success is measured as being able to produce *more* in *less* time, then we Danes are a success. To most people, this success means more work crammed into the same amount of time. How do employees react to this situation? How do they solve this time problem? Many people do so by bringing their work home. Nearly one in two members of Danmarks Jurist- og Økonomforbund (the Association of Danish Lawyers and Economists) bring work home in the evenings and the weekends (*Fyns Stifttidende*, 2004). Others try to cope with the extra workload by going home in the afternoon merely to return to work later in the evening to finish the job. By working like this it still looks as if the tasks have been solved within the normal working hours. Part-time employees are also starting to work overtime, and for many it has become normal to stay a few extra hours each day. All of these different solutions to the time problem are, of course, inappropriate in the long run, because it affects people's leisure time and gives management a wrong perception of the degree of work pressure the employees are labouring under.

Busyness is in our blood. In our everyday lives we try to earn a few extra minutes here and there. What is saved is earned. Many people skip their breaks and eat by the computer while working. That saves thirty minutes on the lunch break. Many people speak on the mobile while driving (although this is, of course, illegal in the UK unless a hands-free system is being used). We are "multi-tasking". Doing several things at the same time saves time—we seem to think. In reality, it often means that we only do things by half. When you are multi-tasking you are not focused on what you are actually doing because you have to focus on several things at once. As a result, it is much easier to make mistakes, forget things, or be injured, because it is all going too fast. A constant fast pace means that both your body and your mind are pushed to the limit. You risk losing track of things and consequently become stressed. In an experiment in the USA, scientists had participants perform several tasks at the same time. The result was a reduction of efficiency by 25–50%, because the participants had to change focus all the time (Hundevadt, 2003).

We are active and busy most of the time. This means, among other things, that we spend less time on social interaction than we did before. Fifteen years ago we spent twice as long being social as we do today (Hundevadt, 2003). We also sleep less than we did earlier. Scientists in the UK and the USA have discovered that we sleep two hours less each night than we did 100 years ago. Within the past fifteen years, the Danes have cut fifteen minutes off their sleeping time. We also spend less time relaxing than we did earlier. In 1990 we spent an average of twenty-five minutes each day relaxing, but today we only spend eight minutes relaxing! If this development continues, relaxing will have totally vanished by the year 2010, or so the writer Kim Hundevadt predicts in his book *Kanten af Kaos* (*The Edge of Chaos*) (*ibid.*). Relaxation will become a thing of the past, which we will merely read about in the history books (*ibid.*).

In a Danish study (Jensen, 2001), adults were asked if they thought that things ought to be moving slower. (The test individuals crossed out more than one answer.) The results were:

53% answered: Yes, definitely;
58% answered: Yes, maybe;
21% answered: No.

According to sociologist Mette Jensen (Jørgensen, 2002) we have become used to being busy and having to rush things all the time. We run around for most of the twenty-four hours in a day, and we cannot do without the fast pace and the excitement. We challenge ourselves by seeing how much of this we are able to take. More and more activities are pushed into the twenty-four hours—we might soon have reached our limit. People often complain about not having enough time, but Mette Jensen hints that it is rather a question of us not getting the most out of the time available to us. We have become increasingly busy through the past couple of years. Within the past twenty years, the "busyness-curve" has risen dramatically. The difference between now and then is that today we are busy all the time. This has several consequences, one of them being stress-related illnesses. The fast pace means that we are unable to relax when we are not working. This is a self-fuelling problem, which leads to the pace becoming even faster both at work and at home. A PhD study of young people's choices and visions in relation to work and family showed that the young people dreamt of a harmonious family life but prioritized their career above this. They organize their family life according to the job (*Berlingske Tidende*, 2003a). A Gallup-poll shows that nearly one in five Danes have changed the amount of time spent with their families in order to spend more time working (*Berlingske Tidende*, 2003b). Work, then, is what is most important to many people. Prioritizing work above family leads to an imbalance between family life and work life. This, according to Mette Jensen, is one of the most serious and challenging problems that societies face today.

Satisfaction with the length of the working week

The Danes are, for the most part, satisfied with the formal working week of thirty-seven hours. A survey done for HK/Privat (a trade union for commercial and clerical employees) shows that Danes do not want a shorter working week (Faber, 2004). This must seem puzzling to the trade unions that, for several years, have fought for the reduction of the working week, longer holidays, and higher wages for their members. Dansk Metal (the Danish trade union for people with mechanical, technical, and electronic knowledge, as well as people working with information technology), for example, is a great advocate of a reduction of the working week to thirty-five hours. The Danes' zeal can be understood in several different ways. One can view the Danes' lack of support for a shorter working week as an expression that they are pressed for time. People have experienced that, although the work hours are reduced, the number of tasks they will have to perform are not. Many people find that it is difficult to get all their work done in thirty-seven hours and therefore think that a thirty-five hour working week is unrealistic. Another explanation might be that many people simply enjoy going to work. At work, our social needs are fulfilled and our colleagues are also our friends. The work even provides a specific reward in the form of wages. In addition, you may even be praised and acknowledged on the basis of your performance. Tasks performed at home are not rewarded, and often the effort is taken for granted by the partner and children. To many people, the job is more interesting than housework and child-rearing. It also turns out that many people feel under pressure at home. A study shows that one in five Danes feel more stressed at home than at work. And one in four feels that they are more in control of their time at work than at home with the family (Jensen, 2001). Maybe we push ourselves more at the end of the workday because we put too great demands on ourselves in relation to what we have to achieve in our spare time. This may also explain why the Danes are generally happy with the thirty-seven hour working week. The home may not be as attractive as it could be.

Besides being satisfied with the length of the working week, Danes are also generally satisfied with their jobs. Two out of three employees are satisfied with their job, and the Danish workplaces receive the highest marks when it comes to education, opportunities for professional and personal development, working conditions, and wages (Lindhardt & Urhskov, 1997).

Success

Today, our identity and success is, to a large degree, connected to our work life. This has not always been the case. In this short historical section we look at how our perception of success and identity has changed throughout time. Going back to the nineteenth century, we find that success was not connected to winning or being the best (Giddens, 1991). One's performance was not measured against what others could perform. Success and performance, however, was connected to an abstract ideal about discipline and self-denial, which were, without doubt, related to Christian ideals.

It was not until the beginning of the twentieth century that success was connected with the will to win. This occurred because ambitious young men now had to compete with their peers for a limited number of positions, as well as for the attention and acknowledgement of their superior. A promotion now depended upon will-power, self-confidence, energy, and initiative. In the following decades up to the 1960s, the family was at the centre of, as well as the most valuable thing in, the life of the individual (Sprankle & Ebel, 1987).

When the women entered the labour market the "nuclear family" was no longer the essence of people's lives. At work, women had an experience of being both seen and heard; they were now getting recognition as well as wages for the work they did, which was something quite new to them. The work of the housewife had not been appreciated in quite the same way. Women now had an identity through their jobs and were more financially independent. The 1980s became a decade in which an individual was equated with his or her professional occupation, more so than at any other time in history. The yuppie culture, with its emphasis on long work hours, gained ground. The yuppie lifestyle was all about material goods, consumption was glamourized, and these people were seen as successful. In the 1990s, as well as today, work took up a lot of time and mental space in most people's lives. Many people identify with their jobs, and this means, among other things, that one's professional role often merges with one's private role.

Identity and dedication

There are other reasons than the merely financial ones why the job plays such an important role in many people's lives. It is commonly accepted throughout Danish society that work is necessary because it creates and maintains identity. Societies, clubs, and the local community do not play the same role in people's lives as they did earlier. This is why many people look for a sense of community in other places. This sense of community is, in our society, related to work. One of the places in which an individual can become a part of something that is greater than himself, and *be* something, is in the workplace. If a person is thriving in his job and is even able to consent to the values and attitudes of the workplace, it becomes even easier to identify with the job. Some people show distinct signs of identifying with their workplace by using the company uniform, or clothes bearing the company logo, outside the job. We live in a culture in which we show who we are through our jobs. This is why our private selves merge with our professional identity. When a person identifies with his work and his qualifications, he is only as good as his last performance. One's own worth is equated with the value of the performance. You are what you can do. This is why work and their performances at the job are so important to so many people. Without work many people feel useless. We see this in the unemployed, who often experience low self-esteem and self-confidence. They feel as if they are not part of the community and feel that they are worth nothing. Many of them say that they feel as if they have lost their identity. The same is true of many people who have retired. We all know the situation when we meet a stranger. The first question is normally: "So what do you do?", meaning, what is your job—your identity? There is a certain amount of security in placing people in a certain box. Knowing people's work identity we seem to know *who* they are. Identity is related to work because work gives us an idea about who we are and what we will be doing in the future. Thus, work creates identity because it creates a degree of continuity in our lives.

One of the explanations of why some people work long hours is that many people are very conscientious and put great demand on themselves. In addition, many employees think that their boss expects a greater effort than is actually the case. In connection with this, dedication is a keyword. Dedication has become a key term when it comes to recruitment, and the word pops up in almost all job advertisements. It is expected as well as demanded that employees are dedicated, because it is perceived as being important to the organization as a whole. The more involved and dedicated an employee is, the better. But how do you show that you really *are* dedicated? One way is to spend a lot of time in the workplace, and maybe even be available, if necessary, in your spare time. This leads to the boundary between work and leisure time becoming blurred. You show dedication, then, by sacrificing yourself for the organization—by doing something out of the ordinary. If work, on the other hand, is not given a high priority in your life, you may easily come across as undedicated, especially if your colleagues put aside their families and spare time for the sake of the job.

That working a lot is important to us, and that it is more than a financial necessity, is seen in several different ways. In a USA survey from the 1980s, an impressive 80% answered "yes" to the question which asked if they would still work if they had just won or inherited enough money to live as comfortably as they had done before. The reasons for this are, according to the Americans who were questioned, that work keeps you occupied and offers you something to interest you. You would feel lost without work, mainly because you would not know how to spend your time (Husén, 1984).

Flow

There are, as I have mentioned, several reasons why some people spend most of their time on work. One reason may be that these people, through their work, experience a pleasurable sensation called flow (Csikszentmihalyi, 1991). We have probably all tried being so engrossed in a certain activity, be it sports, a hobby, a game, or work, that we forgot everything around us because we were so concentrated on what we were doing. This is flow. The state can occur by chance or may be achieved by consciously losing oneself in something you find interesting. One of the requirements for experiencing flow is that you are mentally or physically active, and that the task at hand is sufficiently challenging. There also has to be a balance between your skills and the demands put on you. Watching TV could never result in flow, as you are not active, but merely a passive spectator. There exist many examples of people forgetting to eat or being late for appointments because they were in a state of flow. One such story narrates how half a ceiling had come crashing down while a surgeon was operating. Because he was in a state of flow and everything except the job at hand had been excluded form his mind, he did not notice what had just happened. After the operation he asked why bricks and sheets of ceiling were lying on the floor.

Flow is a pleasurable state and implies a harmonious conscience; for this reason, it is considered a reward in itself. When in a state of flow you are concentrated on one particular thing and everything else is excluded. This means that problems and pain go away during flow. This can be a considerable side effect. If your job is sufficiently challenging, it may provide you with this pleasurable experience of flow. In addition, it may become a refuge if you are burdened with sorrows and worries in your life. Many people may not even be conscious that the pleasurable experience they sometimes have, when deeply lost in their work, is flow. Still, they may try more or less consciously to achieve this state through work. The experience of flow may, therefore, be one of the explanations of why a large number of people work long hours.

It is without a doubt a privilege to have an interesting job, which makes sense to you. The trick is to be able limit the amount of work you can do and to control your own work habits. You should be able to give high priority to other things in your life, instead of getting lost in the job to the point that it eventually takes up all your time.

In the next chapter we examine how it feels when work takes control of your life, and at the characteristics of work addiction. The chapter investigates different thought patterns and explains the symptoms of work addiction. In other words, it examines what exactly work addiction is.

CHAPTER THREE

What is work addiction?

"In the old days, people went home to their wives and children at the end of the day"

(Aja, nine years old)

Physical and mental addiction

Henrik Graversen often experienced a kind of intoxication when he worked seventy hours a week. He got high when endorphin and adrenalin rushed through his body. He never took a holiday, because he became physically ill when he was not working. "It is in my nature to be always in a rush. I like working towards something, but I do not like reaching the goal line, and I am always rushing towards the next." Henrik was addicted to his work. For more than twenty years he worked as a successful IT expert, but one day his body said stop. In the middle of a messy divorce, Henrik started a new job, and that was more than he could cope with.

When he woke up one morning, his energy was gone, and he did not feel like doing anything. Up until that morning Henrik had struggled with an ulcer, anxiety attacks, slips of the memory and shortness of breath, but he had tried to ignore these problems and had continued in the same fast pace. He was absent from his job for four months, due to illness. During a bicycle ride in France, he realized that he was never going back to the IT business. Today he is training to be a woodman. Henrik likes being close to nature, but he is vexed about not being able to work with what he is good at. The illness made him realize that in the future he must be careful not to push himself too hard. [Sonne, 2003]

This example illustrates how work can take control of a person, and how the body may react against it in the end. This part of the book deals with the physical and the mental addiction which together constitute an addiction to work.

Occupational health psychologist Einar Baldursson (2004), who works at the University of Aalborg has, for several years, been using psychotherapy with people suffering from work-related mental problems, including people who could be regarded as workaholics, due to their reactions to stress. He characterizes work addiction as a physical as well as mental addiction, and explains that it is a question of an involvement in work that gets out of control.

You can experience an ecstasy-like physical effect in connection with an intense involvement in your work. In addition it can be an intoxicating experience for the workaholic to seek to create his own success. The job thus brings vigour and excitement into the workaholic's life, just as gambling does for the compulsive gambler. [ibid.]

Baldursson describes workaholics as people who, after periods of having to deal with a considerable work load, become almost addicted to the physiological reactions that follow a tremendous work effort. The person, furthermore, becomes addicted to the experience of self-affirmation that often comes with such an effort.

When the workaholic is in what we call a state of abuse, in which he is working excessively for a long period if time, he will first experience an intellectual intensity. He will feel like he is able to think much faster, and remember a lot more, than [he] would normally do. He may, therefore, go through, analyse, and sort information a lot faster than usual. He will feel much more efficient, and everything is running in top gear. If he continues this intensive work effort, the second phase will set in, in which he will experience being able to focus only on certain tasks shutting out all other sense impressions and outside influences. In this phase he feels as if he can concentrate on and endure much more than he is used to. [*ibid.*]

The psychologist continues:

During both phases you feel like your body performs and feels perfect. You feel no pain, or discomfort. In the third phase this feeling of delight develops into a feeling of sharpened senses, and your experience of sight, hearing and taste feels particularly intense. This is when the actual ecstasy occurs, and signs of self-conceit and delusions of grandeur begin to show themselves. The person feels invincible, and during this phase he loses his sense of reality in relation to his own abilities to cope with the work load. [*ibid.*]

Baldursson compares the workaholics to people who practise extreme sports, because their experiences of ecstasy are very similar. The difference between the two groups of addicts is that the activity in extreme sports is short and physical, whereas the work addiction lasts for weeks or even months. In addition, work addiction involves a high degree of intellectual involvement, because it always necessitates excessive use of mental resources. It is only through this excess use that you can get to the point where the ecstasy manifests itself. In the beginning, stress is almost a side effect of the process. But, gradually, physical and mental reactions to stress become more and more apparent. At the same time, you lose your ability to sense and register your own situation. During this course of events, stress becomes a big part of the person's life and this, paradoxically, increases the tendency to become even more involved in the job. The ecstasies occur less frequently, and many people take on more tasks in the "hope" that they will experience the same feeling of success they had before. Stress is no longer a side effect, but almost becomes a vital necessity for the seriously afflicted workaholic.

According to Baldursson, people are workaholics because it gives them three things:

1. The physiological reactions that occur after a very demanding work-effort (as described above).

2. The particular type of affirmation this self-staging makes possible. Some people feel, for a short while, like a small "god" because of the delusions of grandeur that occur in the third phase (see above).
3. The experience of rising above the ordinary and commonplace everyday life, and getting an extraordinary external acknowledgement, such as a promotion or a cash bonus.

Baldursson explains,

> After a period of intense work the workaholic will often perceive everyday life as dull and monotonous. He starts to miss the ecstasy. Just like people who practise extreme sports, or drug addicts, the workaholic may experience withdrawal symptoms when he does not get his "drug". The first signs that his "system" is beginning to wear down are reactions such as muscle pains, nausea, and headaches. The mental reactions include lack of motivation and energy, along with a feeling of dislike at the thought of having to go get involved in work once more. But then time goes by, and these periods grow farther and farther apart, and slowly a sense of lack occurs, a sense of everyday life being "tedious", and before long he has convinced himself that he is ready for another round. [*ibid.*]

The psychologist continues,

> Through the job the workaholics experience a sense of being "on" and being "important". Something they do not feel they have the opportunity of experiencing in their private lives. They achieve affirmation through their jobs, and at the workplace this affirmation is achieved much easier than at home.

In the people addicted to work, Baldursson sees a pattern, very similar to the pattern of other addicts. They try to convince others that it is only for a period that they experience this increased work load, and that they are in control of the situation, and that they can handle it. They promise to take a holiday—when the pressure of work is lessened. "Both workaholics and alcoholics pretend to be in control of their situation, but in reality it is the work, or the alcohol, that is in control of them," Baldursson concludes.

Physical addiction

Work addiction can be explained by theories of addiction (McMillan, O'Driscoll, Marsh, & Brady, 2001). These theories presume that the addiction is pleasant in the beginning, because it produces positive bodily sensations that make the person continue his behaviour (*ibid.*). The theories of addiction belong either to a medical or a psychological model. The medical model is founded on the assumption that a positive physical experience is connected with the excessive use of mental resources. The psychological model is based on the assumption that there is a mental reward connected with this excessive use. To the drug addict, the taking of the drug is intoxication; to the workaholic, the intoxication, the sense of being "high", occurs when the body is pushed to its limits by several hours of excessive work, every day, for a long period of time. According to several researchers (McMillan, O'Driscoll, Marsh, & Brady, 2001, among others), workaholics experience a physical kick by working hard. They talk of a euphoric state in which the person is operating at a very fast pace, and has an experience of performing his best. The person is not necessarily aware of what is causing this feeling of euphoria. He may, therefore, unconsciously put himself in situations of demanding and intense work pressure and strain. The physical kick is created by the work process, not by the end result.

What happens physically when we push the body, for instance, by working hard, is that we put it in a state of stress. In the beginning this state is both desirable and pleasant, but in the long run it can be damaging to our health. Long periods of stress can lead to illness that, in the worst cases, may result in death. In the beginning you feel as if you have a lot of physical as well as mental energy, and you experience an intense feeling of being alive. This occurs, among other reasons, because the five senses, touch, sight, smell, taste, and hearing, are sharpened. In addition, a part of the brain, the hypothalamus, releases endorphins, which are the body's own morphine. This means that pain is relieved, or completely taken away (Friström, 2003). People who run regularly are familiar with this phenomenon, which is called "runners' high". They admit that they miss this kick, when they are not running. Mountain climbers also get "high" from the production of endorphins that occur in connection with the danger aspect of the sport. If the body produces endorphins on a regular basis, it needs still larger amounts in order to get "high". This may then turn into a vicious circle, in which you push your body further and further. It is not desirable that your body produces endorphin kicks at short intervals, as endorphins, like other drugs, are addictive.

Mental addiction

In addition to the physical kick, the workaholic also experiences an emotional kick. This state is typically achieved in connection with the praise and recognition that come in the wake of a great work effort. It may be the general admiration of friends when you talk of the many hours you spend at work, or it may be praise from your manager and colleagues after a certain performance at work. In these cases, the kick is psychological and not physiological.

The psychological theory of addiction includes the presumption that an excessive use occurs only because of the rewards achieved (McMillan, O'Driscoll, Marsh, & Brady, 2001). In other words, the person experiences one or more advantages by living as he does. The theory of addiction indicates that as long as the advantages of the addiction are greater than the disadvantages, the excessive use will continue. One of the advantages of work addiction might be that the person achieves recognition and maybe even a promotion, followed by an increase in the prestige and the status he enjoys at work. Another reward might be that a potential emotional chaos is kept at bay by concentrating on the job at hand. The distraction of work can help suppress negative emotions such as grief, anger, and fear (Killinger, 1991). The job may, therefore, work as an escape, just like alcohol or a fix does, because it lessens the emotional pain and distances the person from any problems in his private life. If you want a better balance in your life, so that your job does not take up all your time, it may be necessary to confront your emotional or personal problems.

Drugs have the added effect of taking the user from a state of feeling inferior to a state in which he feels that he is special. This can be the decisive motivational factor in relation to continuing the excess use. If you feel as though your work has taken control of you, and if you wish to change this, it is necessary for you to identify the advantages you achieve by living as you do. According to the psychological theory of addiction, a good solution would be to try to achieve the same or similar advantages through more desirable behaviour. One advantage to spending a lot of time at work could be spending time with friends, as our colleagues, in many cases, are also our friends. The solution, then, could be to find equally rewarding friendships outside work, so that you do not have to go to work to see your friends. Having several social networks will also help to create a better balance in your life.

The psychological model is an optimistic one, because it indicates that the behaviour of the workaholic can be replaced by other, more desirable, behaviour. The way the psychological model approaches work addiction is that it is possible to change the patterns that cause the addiction, if the person is motivated to do so. A man who is controlled by his work might, for instance, learn not to work at weekends. All it takes is that the advantages he got from working at the weekends are achieved by other means, or replaced by other advantages. As with other things in our lives, we have to be able to see the advantage of changing something—if we do not see this, we will not be motivated to change our habits and the way we live.

It is still not clear if the workaholic is driven by the physical feeling of being "high", or by the psychological advantages. In order to find an answer to this, studies, including interviews with former and current workaholics, are necessary. But whether the person is chasing the emotional or the physical rewards, the job can be regarded as a means of achieving that goal.

Work addiction impairs the life of the workaholic

One of the problems of work addiction, as with any addiction, is that, to a degree, you become cut off from your emotions and, in the worst cases, lose any sense of your surroundings. You are at risk of gradually turning away from the real world towards your own world (of work).

A travelling machine fitter relates:

When I am in Norway, there is nothing but work in my life. For three to four weeks I am totally cut off from the world around me, and I do nothing but work, I think of work and talk to my colleague about work. My world is simple and my life rather uncomplicated. In the course of a few weeks I forget how to live a normal life. As a result, it takes a while, when I get home, to get into the rhythm of doing the shopping and all the normal everyday things again.

Theories of addiction predict that an addiction will grow worse if different kinds of habits forming behaviour or use of stimulants are continued over a long period of time. The addict will develop a tolerance in relation to his "excessive use", which means that his body will be able to take increasing amounts of stimulants or work. Thus, the body will need still larger amounts in order to experience the kick (Rasmussen, 2004a,b). Bryan Robinson, who is one of the leading experts when it comes to addiction, predicts that this kind of addiction can develop fatally, and that the severely afflicted workaholic is at risk of dying before drawing his pension (Robinson, 1998a). In Japan, the death rate among young males, who are working all the time, is rising. The phenomenon is called *karoshi*, and essentially means a sudden death after a long period of intensive work. We return to this in Chapter Five.

The problem of getting too involved in your work, as with any form of addiction, is that the longer the addiction lasts the more it becomes an integral a part of the individual. Several factors can influence this, and the discussion, among theorists of addiction, deals both with the role of the social environment and the importance of personal, biological, and genetic factors. We look at the importance of these factors, in relation to the development of a work addiction, in Chapter Four.

Characteristics of the workaholic

The people who are addicted to their work are, of course, not all the same, and they all behave in different ways. Diane Fassel is one of the experts on this subject. From material gathered from the first groups of Workaholics Anonymous in the USA, and from interviews with the participants in these meetings, she has described six distinct characteristics of the workaholic (Fassel, 1992). Not all the characteristics will be present in any one individual, but the six characteristics give a general description of the phenomenon. Based on Fassel's work, I explain the six characteristics as follows:

- multiple addictions;
- self-esteem problems;

- external referenting;
- obsessiveness;
- inability to relax;
- denial.

Multiple addictions

A workaholic will usually experience an excessive use of other things besides work. Many addicts will not eat at all during the day, but get by on coffee, cola, or cigarettes. This addiction to caffeine and tobacco is clearly seen at the Workaholics Anonymous meetings, at which the room is filled with smoke and the automatic coffee maker is brewing all night long. Some workaholics are also addicted to alcohol, and are only able to relax after a demanding day if they consume a certain amount of alcohol. Others have a tendency to overeat when they feel stressed. You may thus be addicted to one or more things, besides work, and you risk having several types of addiction dominate your life.

Self-esteem problems

If work has taken control of you, your self-esteem may be constantly changing. Usually, you change between seeing yourself as an extremely competent or an extremely incompetent individual. Thus, many workaholics do not have a realistic image of themselves. The changing self-esteem is one of the reasons why the workaholic often promises more than he can keep, this happens in the periods in which he has too high expectations of his own capabilities. As a result, he lets down a lot of the people around him. This can lead to stress. At times when he experiences a lack of trust in his own abilities he may turn down jobs, which he was more than competent enough to do; he will then come to regret this later on.

The workaholic's unstable sense of self is related to his having difficulties with accepting himself for who he is—including his strengths and weaknesses. As a result he may emphasize and exaggerate his own performances and play down or leave out any mistakes he may have made. He does not expect others to fully accept him, as he does not fully accept himself. This means that he might appear to be an untrustworthy person. If the person is to get away from this pattern of changing self-esteem, it would be helpful if employers did not punish employees for their mistakes, but rather regard them as signs of development and learning. If the knowledge generated by mistakes were shared with the other employees, the whole firm would benefit from it. At the same time, it would prevent others from making the same mistake. Many companies are already using mistakes constructively in this way.

The paradox of work addiction is that a person may experience both a high degree of self-confidence and a low degree of self-esteem at the same time. A workaholic will often have high self-confidence when it comes to his ability to do his job; this self-confidence will grow as the tasks become more and more difficult. It is, thus, possible for a person to see himself as a competent businessman, sportsman, or teacher without feeling valuable as a person. While self-confidence is centred on performances and skills, self-esteem is the fundamental feeling of being worth something as a human being, independent of what you can do. A person with a healthy feeling of self-esteem will seldom have problems with low self-confidence, whereas high self-confidence does not automatically lead to high self-esteem. The severely afflicted workaholics who have low self-esteem may feel insecure and be critical of themselves. Typically, they seem like self-assured people on the outside, but the controlled behaviour and appearance may be a façade, covering for a feeling of low self-esteem.

External referenting

Most of us are affected by what other people think of us. Some people, however, are so focused on the signals other people send out that they let their lives be controlled by other people's opinions. You are subject to external referenting when you look to your surroundings for signs of how you should feel and behave. It is usually people with some degree of low self-esteem who are subject to external referenting.

There are several reasons why a person becomes subjected external referenting. One of them is growing up in a dysfunctional family, in which one or both parents are addicts or mentally ill. In such families the children spend a lot of time trying to read the adults, and adapt to the specific circumstances in the home. If the alcoholic dad comes home drunk, the child will, from the noises he is making, be able to tell if he is aggressive or not. The child will adapt to the situation by, for example, going to bed and pretending to be asleep, to avoid provoking the father and becoming a victim of violence. This "chameleon strategy" is crucial for the survival of the children, but it is unfortunate because the children ignore their own feelings and needs, and instead adapt themselves to the behaviour of others.

If you have grown up in a dysfunctional family, you will have been "trained" to constantly repress your own needs and satisfy the needs of others. This kind of upbringing provides the conditions for developing a work addiction later in life, because, by working, the person achieves praise and recognition for his performances, and thereby satisfies the parents, the teacher, or the manager. Praise and recognition might be what the person strives for, and the addict may aim at a promotion because he will thus achieve respect from others. He may not feel accepted for who he *is*, but rather for what he *does*.

Companies rarely ask that an employee works excessively, or that he performs something out of the ordinary. In most cases, it is the workaholic himself who thinks that others expect him to work extremely hard. A workaholic thrives on reactions to his performances and judges himself on the basis of these reactions. Therefore, it is important that his performances be visible. If they are not visible, the workaholic may attract attention to what he has accomplished, in order to make his productivity visible. In order to feel comfortable he needs to be doing something productive, such as work. He will, therefore, often take on too many assignments at work, and push himself too hard in order to have time to do everything. All his activity and inactivity is justified in relation to his work. If the workaholic takes a half-hour nap, he will justify it to himself and others by saying that he was more productive afterwards. Relaxation is primarily a tool used to optimize his work effort.

If you ask a person who spends most of his time on his job how he is *feeling*, he will often tell you what he is *doing*. Workaholics like to talk about their jobs and their accomplishments. However, they seldom tell you what is going on inside them—what they think and how they feel. It is generally easier for them to relate to actions than emotions.

The workaholic's actions are often controlled by circumstances outside himself, instead of by his own feelings and needs; this shows itself in several ways. He might, for instance, develop the habit of making lots of long lists of everything he has to do. In extreme cases, spending time with his partner and playing with his children are added to the list of things to do. Specific days of the weeks are appointed for so-called "quality time" with the children. This, however, may be unfortunate if the children do not want to play on Wednesday and Thursday from 5 to 6 p.m., as this may be the only time set aside for this activity. For some people, their lists become almost an obsession. In those cases, the workaholic is at risk of being controlled by the lists, as they tell him what to do. This will cause the spontaneity to disappear from the person's life, so that he will only do the things on the list. The following case is an example of this.

> Heather, who was a teacher, had a folder full of "to do" lists. The lists were divided into "urgent", "today", "long-term projects", "family", "friends", "children", and "phone", including a list for each of the classes she taught. Every time she remembered something she had to do, whether it was important or not, she wrote it down. Heather always brought the "to do" lists with her. She would take them out wherever she was, to write something down, cross something out, and read what she had to do next. If she had finished one list she quickly made a new one, with the same heading, and added a few points. In this way she made sure she was always kept busy, and she was always rushing from one activity to the next. Heather knew that her mania had grown out of proportion, and occasionally she would laugh at herself, saying, "If I don't show up for work one day it is because it is not on my 'to do' list."

For Heather, and for others who let their day be dominated by "to do" lists, life becomes an endless row of activities that they have to get through. They focus only on the future, and the person is always "going somewhere" instead of being present in the moment.

Obsessiveness

If work has taken control of you, then your work habits have got out of control and you probably always feel the need to be

working. While the ones who are not addicted to work try to be efficient and finish the job, the workaholic is always looking for new
tasks and creates work for himself. He is always thinking about his
job and, in the worst cases, he is obsessed by work. For this reason,
the workaholic is almost always preoccupied with his job—physically as well as mentally. It is difficult for him to let go of the job,
and it follows him wherever he goes: when he is driving his car, in
the middle of a conversation, watching TV, taking a shower or lying
in his bed, he is thinking about his job. As a result, he never truly
unwinds. If you are constantly preoccupied with your job, it may
be downright dangerous in several situations. You may drive
through a red light at an intersection, or leave the iron on, because
you are not present mentally, only physically. Some workaholics are
preoccupied with how many hours they work. They try to exceed
their own boundary and set a new record in the numbers of hours
they work in a day, or a week. They often compete against themselves and their colleagues. The compulsive addict is prone to
working at a fast pace. The frenzied pace does not necessarily mean
that he is more efficient, as mistakes and accidents will happen
when the pace is too fast. Documents will go missing, things are
knocked over, and appointments are forgotten, because everything
happens too fast. As a result, workaholics are not the efficient
employees one would expect them to be.

Inability to relax

The tendency towards being too involved in work that characterizes the workaholic is related to him being unable to relax. Being a
workaholic, you are always on your feet, working. With a constantly high level of adrenalin in the body, it is difficult to relax and
to fall asleep at night. You constantly feel as if you should be doing
something, and you keep yourself occupied by adding new tasks to
your list of things to do. The more addicted to work you are, the
more restless you will become when you are not working. For the
severely afflicted workaholic, it will provoke anxiety not to be
doing anything. If these people ever go on holiday, they will take
some work with them and come up with excuses as to why they
have to spend time on it.

Peter, who was the office manager in a large company, had—to the regret of his wife—not been on holiday for three years in a row. The company had merged with another company and there was always some work that demanded his presence. Peter had promised his wife Helen that this year they would go on holiday to Greece for a week. Helen was looking forward to them finally spending a whole week together, but Peter became more and more agitated as the day of departure drew near.

The week before the holiday he worked until 11 p.m. every night. Still he did not feel as if he had done everything he ought to have done, and he brought his laptop and some paperwork on holiday. Just in case it rained. On the plane he did not dare tell Helen that he had brought some work with him, but at the same time he was already itching to get the documents out, and make the most of the time. The first day everything was fine, and they spent the day sightseeing and enjoying good food, but at night Peter could not sleep. He kept thinking of the colleagues back home, and whether they would manage without him. The next day he was restless and could not relax. On the third day he stayed in bed, saying that he was ill. When Helen had gone to the beach, he sneaked over to the neighbouring hotel, where he could go on the Internet. What a relief finally to be in touch with the company and answering the e-mails that were waiting for him! The next day went by in the same manner.

Peter admitted to Helen that he had been working. Her disappointment and anger resulted in a big quarrel. Peter felt guilty towards his wife, but work meant everything to him. Besides, he was convinced that his colleagues could not manage without him. During the last days of the holiday, Peter had his mobile phone turned on and his colleagues phoned him regularly.

One of the ways you can protect yourself from stress is to relax and unwind by taking up a hobby or seeing family and friends in your spare time. The workaholic's inability to relax is one of the most serious symptoms, because lack of relaxation does not allow the body and mind to recover and "recharge" its batteries.

Denial

Common to all types of addiction is the defence mechanism denial. Being in denial means that the addict cannot, and often will not, admit that he has a problem. Being in denial protects the person from facing reality and thereby being forced to change his ways. People will usually try to hide an addiction, because they are embarrassed that they are not in control of themselves. The opposite is often the case with the workaholics. They will frequently tell, at family gatherings and in the media, how their lives consist of nothing but work. The reason is that we live in a culture of high work morals in which we admire people who work a lot.

Denial can be described as the addict's worst enemy, as it prevents him from admitting his addiction, and, consequently, acting to prevent it. If the workaholic is to achieve a better balance in his life, the first and most important step is to admit that work has taken control of him.

The six characteristics of work addiction are interconnected, and some of them even overlap. The habit of promising more than one can deliver, for example, is connected not only with the changing self-image that leads the addict to overestimate his own capabilities, but also to his being subject to an external locus of control that is characterized by his wish to please others. Low self-respect is thus connected to this subjection to an external locus of control, which leads the person to seek to please others instead of himself. In addition, the compulsive behaviour makes the person incapable of relaxing. The six characteristics can be difficult to separate, as they all affect each other.

The rigid thinking that relates to workaholism

In addition to the six characteristics mentioned above, a number of thought patterns are also typical of workaholics. In his studies, Robinson, who, as mentioned earlier, is one of the leading experts on the subject, has compared workaholics with non-addicts and discovered that the workaholics are driven by distinct ways of thinking (Robinson, 1998a). In other words, they have a characteristic cognitive pattern. The cognitive pattern contributes to the understanding of what work addiction is, and it shows us in what areas the workaholics differ from other people. According to Robinson, twelve types of rigid thinking characterize the workaholic's thought patterns and are present in each workaholic to varying degrees. It is important to understand these thought patterns, because they are closely linked to emotions and behaviour. The cognitive pattern thus contributes to a more nuanced image of work addiction. It is important, however, to emphasize that the individual workaholic does not necessarily display all of these types of thinking. The twelve thought patterns are explained as follows, based on Robinson's work.

Perfectionistic thinking is a dominating thought pattern with many people. If you are too involved in your work, you will often have a high standard of perfection and demand a lot from yourself and the people around you. This perfectionism means that you will seldom be satisfied with your own accomplishments, because you always think that things could have been done better. The perfectionist thinking may result in the workaholic feeling inadequate. The workaholic may, as mentioned earlier, have high self-confidence when it comes to the job, but may at the same time have low self-esteem, because he does not feel adequate on a deeper level. He attempts to alleviate the low self-esteem by trying to be perfect.

All-or-nothing thinking is seen in a large number of people, and is characteristic of the workaholic. This form of thinking is related to the fact that it is difficult to prioritize several areas of your life equally if the job takes up most of your life. If work is dominating your life, you will often feel that you have to prioritize either your career or your family. It often becomes a question of prioritizing either one area or another instead of prioritizing both. This is the reason why many people feel they should commit themselves completely to the job and spend more time at work, or, at the opposite end of the scale, that they should renounce work completely.

Telescopic thinking is a thought pattern that may influence some people. This cognitive pattern leads you to be prone to focus on, and enlarge, any negative experiences. This might impair a person's self-esteem. If a workaholic is criticized by his manager, he might begin to worry that he will soon be fired. At the same time, the workaholic has a tendency to ignore facts that could increase his self-esteem. If he is evaluated favourably by a client or receives positive feedback from his colleagues, he may not attribute any importance to it.

Blurred-boundary thinking is another characteristic thought pattern found in workaholics. It refers to the person not being aware of his own limits, and, as a consequence, he might have difficulty in laying down boundaries for himself. It is difficult for him to express when he finds something unacceptable. One example of his blurred-boundary thinking is the fact that he rarely takes a day off from work. He cannot draw the line and set boundaries for his work, and finds it difficult to know when it is all right to do something besides work.

People-pleasing thinking means that you want to please other people, so that they will like you. A workaholic may take on more than he can handle because he wants to please his manager. He also wants to please his family, and makes repeated promises that he will come home early, or take the weekend off, in order for the whole family to spend time together. As his work has top priority, the result is often that the family will be disappointed, because he cannot keep his promises. Thus, the workaholic has difficulty living up to his own ambition of pleasing others.

Pessimistic thinking affects the workaholic in a way that he sees his life as chaotic and stressful. He thinks he must stay alert and keep working in order not to risk getting behind.

Helpless thinking means that you feel helpless to change the way you live your life. You might be racing against the clock, but feel there is nothing you can do to slow down or change your situation. Your work life and your family life may be unsatisfying, but you feel unable to change things.

Self-victimized thinking is characterized by the person seeing himself as a victim and not in control of his own life. Being a workaholic, you might see yourself as the victim of external circumstances, such as the conditions at the workplace, which you feel you cannot change. You feel a victim of the demands of society, your boss, and your family. *You* have to do it all and nobody gives you a break.

Resistance thinking is a cognitive pattern that leads you to see obstacles everywhere in your life. If you are addicted to your work, to some degree, you are inclined to view life as a struggle, in which there is always some obstacle to be overcome, and tasks to be done. You fight yourself, as well as others, in order to overcome what feels like resistance.

Wishful thinking is when we dream of something—which most of us do. Wishful thinking is an extension of the workaholic seeing his life as stressful and chaotic. He sometimes dreams that the situation will change, and wish that this external change will help him to change his life. He may fantasize about winning in the lottery and lying in a hammock, on a palm beach, far away from the stressful life he now leads.

Serious thinking means that your thinking is serious. This way of thinking makes the workaholic incapable of taking time off, and being unproductive. The more addicted you are, the less involved you become in activities that have as their sole purpose amusement or entertainment, as is the case with various games. If a workaholic does practise some kind of sport, it is often a competitive one.

Externalized thinking means that you are orientated towards your surroundings. You will typically focus on what other people think and mean, and on what they expect of you. Therefore, you try to create visible work results for the purpose of showing your worth. This thought process characterizes the workaholic.

In addition to these thought patterns, we find several physical and emotional symptoms that characterize the workaholic. These are introduced in the next section.

The symptoms of work addiction

Robinson (1998a) has compared workaholics with people who are not addicted to their work, and he found that the addicts are frequently suffering from different physical and behavioural symptoms. These symptoms, mentioned in random order in Table 1, can be viewed as warnings of work addiction (*ibid.*, p. 52).

Almost all of these symptoms are, besides being danger signals of work addiction, symptoms of stress. If you experience one or more of these symptoms you should consider what might be causing them. If the symptoms are severe and occur over a long period of time, it may be an indication that you are suffering from a severe case of stress or work addiction. We return to the subject of stress in Chapter Five.

Table 1. Symptoms of addiction to work.

Physical symptoms	Behavioural symptoms
Headaches	Temper outbursts
Fatigue	Restlessness
Allergies	Insomnia
Indigestion	Difficulty relaxing
Stomach-aches	Hyperactivity
Ulcers	Irritability and impatience
Chest pain	Forgetfulness
Shortness of breath	Difficulty concentrating
Nervous tics	Boredom
Dizziness	Mood swings (from euphoria to depression)

Three types of workaholic

Not all workaholics behave the same way. American researchers (Scott, Moore, & Miceli, 1997) have identified three types of workaholic, who each display different characteristics as well as a set of unique, relatively stable, behavioural patterns. The different characteristics and behavioural patterns do not exclude each other, and, in reality, the workaholic can be a combination of two or all three types.

The compulsive type usually works more hours than he has planned. He rarely goes on holiday, and he is inclined to bring his work on holiday if he actually does go. The compulsive type is often aware that he spends too much time at work, but still he is not able to reduce his work hours because he has a tendency to experience a diffuse anxiety when he is not working. Internal and external busyness is characteristic of this type, which means that the person is often working at a frenzied pace. Several activities are done at the same time, in order to save time. He may, for instance, be on the phone, and writing e-mails at the same time. The compulsive is the most melancholy of the three types. He is usually not particularly happy about his job, and shows only a limited degree of creativity. He will typically continue working despite social or health problems, such as symptoms of stress. He will continue working despite discomfort, because he becomes anxious when he is *not* working. The compulsive type feels that he has to work all the time, in order to avoid anxiety—hence the label "compulsive". You might say that this type is caught in a work trap, and that he locks himself into an inappropriate work pattern in which he tries to solve the problem of anxiety by working. The person may act this way because he has been severely criticized and punished for being lazy earlier on in this life. Inactivity in adulthood may thus create an unconscious fear of being punished. This might be the reason why this type is always working (Nielsen, 1997).

The perfectionist type can, like the compulsive, be characterized by anxiety and stress in his work life. This individual, most of the time, finds himself in a working *process* caused by his perfectionist characteristics. Perfectionism is the main reason why this individual is often unproductive. He has a tendency to alternate between periods of intense work efforts and passivity and the delaying of tasks caused by his fear of making mistakes. Contrary to the compulsive type, who finds it difficult to take time off because of anxiety, the perfectionist does not feel any anxiety or discomfort when he is not working. This type, however, is afraid of not having done his work properly; therefore, he finds it difficult to finish a job and go home. The perfectionist is, furthermore, characterized by focusing on details and rules, with the use of lists. In addition, this individual is often dissatisfied with himself and his job. For the perfectionist workaholic, work and productivity are usually more important than leisure time activities and friendships. If this type participates in games, he will be driven by his aggressive instinct, and controlled by his perfectionism (Killinger, 1991). This means that sports and recreations quickly become competitive when this person participates. This competitiveness also shows itself in the workplace, in which he, contrary to the compulsive type, can appear hostile towards his colleagues in his efforts to be the best. This can make it difficult for this type to be part of a team.

The perfectionist wants to get credit for the result of the work effort; at the same time, his colleagues might find it difficult to deal with his perfectionism. A bad relationship with one's colleagues, caused by perfectionism, might result in further efforts to become perfect. This, then, becomes a self-fuelling negative pattern that makes the situation worse for the addict. The reason for the addict to display this behaviour pattern might be that he has been the subject of severe criticism in his childhood, for example, in connection with school work. He may also have achieved praise and acknowledgement when his (school) work, in the eyes of his parents, was satisfactory. Thus, the motivation for working all the time may be to achieve praise and recognition and to avoid criticism (Nielsen, 1997). One could also imagine that this type of behaviour is the product of the person not feeling in control of his work, or his life in general.

The ambitious type focuses on his performance and has a strong career identity. This type spends as much time working as the two other types; however, he is driven by his desire to perform and his wish to ascend the career ladder. When this individual is promoted, and his career is going in the right direction, he has an experience of work joy. He spends a lot of time thinking about his job and does more than is expected of him; at the same time, he is able to take time off without feeling physically or mentally ill. The ambitious type is more creative and better at working in a team than the other two types. However, he is often intolerant of colleagues who do not work as much as he does. One imagines that the values of the ambitious type, which have to do with success, are founded much earlier in life. He might, thus, be socialized into thinking that people are valuable if they are successful in their work lives and go far in their careers. For this reason, this individual might be driven by an unconscious fear of being worthless in his own eyes and in the eyes of others (Nielsen, 1997).

So far, no studies have shown which types of education might apply to the three types, or what kinds of job they might be found in. But the ambitious type will most likely be found in jobs in which his performances are measurable, and in which he finds a "career ladder" he can ascend. As mentioned above, the individual workaholic may be one of these three types, or he may be a combination of two or three types.

The following is an example of a woman who is a combination of the compulsive, the perfectionist, and the ambitious type.

> Susan is forty-nine years old, and works with mentally handicapped people in a group home. She is very fond of her work, which she calls her hobby. "My job is incredibly exciting and I feel very privileged to be able to work with something that I am truly enthusiastic about." Susan is very involved in her work. She does not want to do things by half and, as a result, she works more hours than is expected of her. Her manager calls her "200%", among other things, because she works one

hour over time nearly every day. "Time flies when I'm there, but that means that I do not have time for all the things I want to do when I get home. In the evenings I am so tired that I haven't the energy to do anything. In the end, I fall asleep on the sofa—even though I make lists of all the things I want to do at work, and at home."

Susan is never truly "off-duty". When she is at home, she thinks about work, and she will often wake up in the middle of the night thinking about the residents at the home. At weekends she often phones up her colleagues or reads specialist literature related to her work. "I'm not good at taking time off. The last time I had holiday, I was unable to relax at all. I called work several times, because I wanted to know what was going on. After a week off I was looking forward to going back to work. Two weeks was much too long for me to be away." Susan's husband is worried about her health, and reminds her that she has to take care of herself. On one occasion her body did actually say stop. For a long period Susan felt chronically tired, her immune system was broken down, and she was constantly ill. Now, she does breathing exercises every day, and is conscious of eating healthily, to avoid another episode like that.

Most of Susan's colleagues work more than they need to. They almost never take time off in lieu of payment, as they have no opportunity to do so. They are always busy, and never have time for breaks. They usually eat while working. Susan admits that the hectic work pattern makes her stressed. As a result, she often forgets things, at work as well as at home. In addition she can feel irritable and find it difficult to concentrate when she spends time with her family. "I do not like the term workaholic, but it *is* an addiction . . ." She admits that one of the advantages to being at work is that she does not have time to think about any problems she might have at home.

Despite the hectic workday, the symptoms of stress, and the lack of free time, Susan has no definite plans to make changes in her life. "I know that my work takes up too much of my time. I would like to have more spare time, so I could cultivate my garden and start running again—I miss those things. I dream of living a simple life without having to worry so much, but I have asked to get more hours at work and soon I will have to start on doing supplementary training, as well as work."

The risk of work addiction

Do you have healthy work habits, or are you becoming addicted to your job? Complete the Work Addiction Risk Test (WART) (Table 2)

Table 2.   The Work Addiction Risk Test.

1.   I prefer to do most things myself rather than ask for help.
2.   I get impatient when I have to wait for someone else or when something takes too long.
3.   I seem to be in a hurry and racing against the clock.
4.   I get irritated when I am interrupted while I am in the middle of something.
5.   I stay busy and keep many irons in the fire.
6.   I find myself doing two or three things at one time, such as eating lunch and writing a memo while talking on the telephone.
7.   I over commit myself by biting off more than I can chew.
8.   I feel guilty when I am not working on something.
9.   It's important that I see the concrete results of what I do.
10. I am more interested in the final result of my work than in the process.
11. Things just never seem to move fast enough or get done fast enough for me.
12. I lose my temper when things don't go my way or work out to suit me.
13. I ask the same question over again, without realizing it after I've already been given the answer once.
14. I spend a lot of time mentally planning and thinking about future events while tuning out the here and now.
15. I find myself continuing to work after my coworkers have called it quits.
16. I get angry when people don't meet my standards of perfection.
17. I get upset when I am in situations where I cannot be in control.
18. I tend to put myself under pressure from self-imposed deadlines when I work.
19. It is hard for me to relax when I'm not working.
20   I spend more time working than socializing with friends, or on hobbies or leisure activities.
21. I dive into projects to get a head start before all the phases have been finalized.
22. I get upset with myself for making even the smallest mistake.
23. I put more thought, time, and energy into my work than I do into my relationships with loved ones and friends.
24. I forget, ignore, or minimize celebrations such as birthdays, reunions, anniversaries, or holidays.
25. I make important decisions before I have all the facts and have a chance to think them through.

Total points: _____

SCORING:

to see if you have reasons to worry. The test is internationally recognized and was developed by Bryan Robinson (1998a, p. 52).

Rate yourself on each of the statements in the table, using the rating scale of 1 (never true), 2 (sometimes true), 3 (often true), and 4 (always true). Put the number that best describes your work habits in the blank space beside each statement. After you have responded to all twenty-five statements, add up the numbers to the right of the statements for your total score. The highest score is 100; the lowest possible is 25. The higher the score, the more likely you are to be a workaholic. The lower your score, the less likely you are to be a workaholic.

For clinical use, scores on the WART are divided into three ranges; those scoring in the upper third (67–100) are considered highly workaholic. If you scored in this range, it could mean that you are on your way to burn-out, and new research suggests that family members may be experiencing emotional repercussions as well.

Those scoring in the middle range (57–66) are considered mildly workaholic. If you scored in this range, there is hope. With acceptance and modifications, you and your loved ones can prevent negative lasting effects.

Those scoring in the lowest range (25–56) are considered not workaholic. If you scored in this range, you probably are an efficient worker instead of a workaholic. You needn't worry that your work style will negatively affect yourself or others.

CHAPTER FOUR

What causes work addiction?

They intoxicate themselves with work so they won't see how they really are.

(Aldous Huxley, quoted in Robinson, 1998a, p. 232)

Some people experience work addiction while others go through life without ever experiencing this. What makes some people develop workaholism? A number of experts have tried to answer this question. They have approached it from different angles and have studied different aspects of work addiction to find out what causes it. It turns out that several things come into play, and that different circumstances increase one's risk of becoming addicted to work. This is why experts can give no single explanation for what causes an addiction to work. In this chapter, I take a closer look at some of the circumstances that determine whether a person develops this type of addiction.

Personality

Several studies have been performed on the subject of work addiction. Most of these studies show that the phenomenon is closely related to personality. Researchers have discovered that certain characteristics are generally present in people who are workaholics. Work addiction, then, is explained as an expression of certain characteristics (McMillan, O'Driscoll, Marsh, & Brady, 2001).

Characteristics

The characteristics that make up the foundation of the development of a work addiction are (Clark, Livesley, Schroeder, & Irish, 1996):

- compulsive tendencies;
- being "obsessed" by something;
- a high level of energy.

Compulsive tendencies mean that the individual is not able to refrain from performing specific actions. In the case of the workaholic, it is typically work that the person finds difficult to let alone. Therefore, it is work that commands the power. He will often continue working despite of fatigue or illness, because he experiences an internal unrest and anxiety when he is not working. The compulsive type, described on pp. 39–40, is an example of this type of behaviour. The compulsive tendencies might also be thoughts that keep haunting the person. Thoughts about the job may infest the person's mind to the point that it may be difficult for him to think of anything else, no matter what he is doing. He may feel, therefore, that he is not in control of himself, because he is not in control of his mind and thoughts. He is at the mercy of his thoughts, and they may plague him, meaning that he is never "off" work because he is always there mentally. Being obsessed by something—in this case work—also means that you are controlled by something outside yourself, so that you feel as though you are not in control of your own life. You are unable to let go of the job and have to be working all the time. A high level of energy indicates that you are very busy and find it difficult to sit still. Because of this particular characteristic, one of the researchers who consider work addiction as something positive and as an advantage, argues that workaholics are simply people who have more energy than the rest of us (Machlowitz, 1980).

The perfectionist—unable to delegate

Experts in the field have also found that workaholics are often perfectionists and that they have a tendency not to delegate tasks to others. The perfectionism shows itself through the individual wanting to perform tasks to perfection. He or she will focus on details and is typically nervous about making mistakes. Many perfectionists will find it difficult to finish a project and often take a long time doing so. (The perfectionist is described as one of the three types of workaholics in Chapter Three, pp. 40–41). The tendency of not being willing to delegate tasks to co-workers may be related to the fact that the workaholic is unconsciously trying to make sure that there is always something for him to do (Spence & Robbins, 1992). By delegating tasks to others, you will not have the same degree of control over how the tasks are performed. The knowledge you gain from doing all the tasks yourself may give you a certain amount of power in the workplace. It may even lead you to acquire a certain position, and you may become an important asset for the company as a whole. It is therefore possible to make oneself indispensable by not delegating tasks. This, however, will trap you in a vicious circle in which you generate more and more work for yourself.

The characteristics described above are seen in most workaholics and therefore form the basis of the explanation of this type of addiction. In some cases, a combination of these characteristics will occur. The characteristics are found in all sorts of different people and with individuals from all sectors of society (McMillan, O'Driscoll, Marsh, & Brady, 2001).

In addition to the influence of personality, one's environment also plays an important part in the development of an addiction to work (*ibid.*). You might, therefore, be predisposed to develop a work addiction because of certain characteristics in your personality, but your environment may prevent it from ever happening. Having a partner who insists that you do not work in the evenings and that you take the whole weekend off might prevent you from losing yourself to your work. Conversely, your environment might also lay the foundation for the development of the addiction to work. If your personality makes you more susceptible than others to being controlled by your job, it may be crucial whether you work in a company with many workaholics on the payroll. If you do get a job like that, your colleagues may be "infectious", which may lead you to spend all your time at work. Finally, the environment may also maintain the work addiction. If conflicts occur within the family, which are not solved immediately, it is easy to continue along the same line and bury oneself in the work, thereby avoiding uncomfortable confrontations at home. In this way, excessive involvement in the job is maintained.

There are, then, several conditions that come into play to determine whether a person develops an addiction to work. Seen collectively, it is a correlation between personality and environment.

Type A personality

Earlier on, experts equated work addiction with the so-called Type A personality, because they thought that these two phenomena were identical (Spence, Helmreich, & Pred, 1987). However, it was later discovered that they were, in fact, not identical (Perez-Prada, 1996). It is true that many people who are addicted to their work display the Type A personality (Burke, 2001), which has nothing to do with how good you are at getting out of bed in the morning.

Type A personalities are characterized by leading hectic and busy lives (Nielsen, 1999). They always seem to be pressed for time and are racing against the clock no matter what they are doing. Type A persons are thus impatient and find it difficult to relax. They are ambitious and are always competing against themselves as well as others. Type A will change queues several times in the supermarket, while repeatedly looking at his or her watch and sighing with irritation over always choosing the slow cash register. We experience them honking their horns and working themselves up in traffic when others—according to them—are not moving fast enough. The worst you can do to them is to make them wait; they will be drumming their fingers and be unable to stand still if they have nothing to do. This type of behaviour leads them to stress themselves, as well as others. Type A personalities are easily stressed and get frustrated easily. They are always trying to convince others that they are good enough. This explains their dedication to their work and the fact that they focus so much on performance. Another aspect of their personality is that they can be hot-tempered and hostile towards other people (*ibid.*).

The Type A phenomenon was discovered by accident. Two heart specialists discovered that the chairs in their waiting room were only worn on the edge. They wondered if their heart patients were particularly restless and always sat on the edge of their seats in order to be able to move on quickly. In order to examine this, they came up with a questionnaire that measures how hectic, impatient, and hostile a person is. They called individuals with a high score Type A, and individuals with a low score Type B. Type B is the opposite of Type A, and is not competitive. Type B is characterized by being calm and relaxed. From the questionnaire, researchers could conclude that there is a clear connection between behaviour and heart disease. Studies have shown that twice as many Type A individuals are suffering from heart disease, compared with Type B (*ibid.*). In the test, scientists made sure that the two groups were alike when it came to blood pressure and cholesterol and that they had the same eating, exercise, and smoking habits. By doing this, scientists excluded an unhealthy lifestyle as the cause of the heart attacks. It is, then, the behaviour of the Type A personality that is damaging to their health. It has turned out that it is the hostility and the anger, rather than the hectic lifestyle, which is dangerous in the Type A personality and increases the risk of heart disease (*ibid.*).

Type A behaviour in the next generation

The positive thing, though, is that Type A individuals can actually *learn* to behave differently. If they are motivated, they can become less stressed and more relaxed through exercise. But they need help from others, as the behavioural patterns of the Type A personality have become an integral part of them because they have typically been behaving like this for several years. In children as young as 10–14 years, the Type A personality can be detected, so it is a life-long behavioural pattern that needs to be changed. Studies show that we learn Type A behaviour from our parents, and that it is not something we are born with (Nielsen, 1999). Twelve-year-old boys were instructed by their fathers in completing a task. The fathers were behaving in a typical Type A manner: they ordered their sons about, pushed them to do their best, and became angry when the boys made mistakes. After the test it was very important for the fathers to know the results. Another group of boys, who were not Type A individuals, solved the same task with their fathers, who, unlike the first group, were relaxed and saw the test more as a game. These fathers were not particularly interested in the result of the test (*ibid.*). The test is a witness to the fact that the unhealthy, Type A behaviour is passed on to the next generation, because children tend to copy the behaviour of their parents.

Children are not only influenced by their parents, but also by the culture in which they live. Our culture could be described as performance and competition orientated. The pace is fast in several areas, leading to stress. This is why society also plays an important part in the development of Type A individuals.

Being a Type A person is, of course, not all negative. Being ambitious and performance orientated are characteristics that may give the individual great satisfaction when a goal is achieved. Unfortunately, Type A people will often rush along to the next task, never enjoying the result of their efforts.

Workaholics and Type A individuals have several things in common. The industry, as well as the competitiveness and the performance orientation, are characteristic of both. In addition, the workaholic may also be hectic and feel pressed for time. Like many other people, some workaholics are also hot-tempered and hostile towards others. And many of them have, as mentioned, a Type A personality; hence, a description of this type of personality may help shed some light on the behaviour of the workaholic.

The importance of environment

"The environment" is the broad term we use for our surroundings. When speaking of a person's environment, it may be both the near surroundings, such as the family, or the overall environment, such as society. In this section we take a closer look at the importance of environment in the development of a work addiction. We start by looking at the surroundings closest to the individual and end by looking at the overall environment.

The influence of the parents

We are influenced from many different directions throughout our childhood and adolescence. Several people influence the kind of people we grow up to be. The people who play a big part in our development of our personality are our parents and our closest relatives. Their attitudes and behaviour, thus, influence our social norms and values as well as our behaviour. In our childhood, our parents are important role models, and the way they live their lives can have a profound impact on the way we live our lives as adults.

In childhood, parents will often unconsciously promote certain behavioural patterns in the child that meet the parents' needs. At the same time, behavioural patterns that do not meet these needs are dismissed (Weinberg & Mauksch, 1991). Maybe the parents like it when the house is peaceful, and therefore praise the children when they are quietly doing their homework. In addition, parents who like peace and quiet may reject or scold the child if it is noisy. In this way, the parents are influencing the child to behave in a certain way which satisfies them.

Studies have been made of the part the parents play in relation to the later development of work addiction in a person (Carroll & Robinson, 2000; Robinson & Chase, 2001). Researchers have compared the behavioural patterns of children whose parents are suffering from a severe addiction to work with the children of alcoholics, because there are several similarities between these two groups in respect of the change of responsibility from one individual to another. The studies show that children of alcoholics, as well as children of workaholics, are at greater risk of becoming addicted themselves as adults (Robinson & Chase, 2001). This is due to the fact that these children, more so than other children, copy the behaviour of their parents (*ibid.*; Carroll & Robinson, 2000). In another study, adults whose parents had been either workaholics or alcoholics assessed their own level of parentification. The children of workaholics shoved more signs of parentification than the children of alcoholics (Robinson & Chase, 2001). Parentification means that the child is behaving as a parent towards other members of the family. The child ignores its own needs for attention, comfort, and guidance in order to meet the emotional needs of other family members (Carroll & Robinson, 2000).

Children living in families with an alcoholic or workaholic are prompted, in several cases, to act as adults (Robinson & Chase, 2001). It may be the case that the alcoholic or the workaholic is physically absent from the home and an "adult" is therefore needed to perform chores around the house and take care of the children. In such cases, the child may assume the role of the adult and act as a parent to his or her siblings. Another case could be one in which the parent who is not experiencing a problem with addiction is not getting his or her need for grown-up contact satisfied, because the partner is mentally and emotionally absent, either because of alcohol or too much work. In situations like this, he or she may involve the child in problems pertaining to adulthood. The parent's need for them may give these children some power and influence within the family. It may, however, also lead the child to take on the responsibility of an adult, which, on account of its age, it is not mature enough to handle. Children who display parentification are often appreciated for *what* they do rather than for *who* they are (Carroll & Robinson, 2000). This means that these children often become more focused on showing how good they are at something. This may be caused by a combination of high expectations on the part of the parents and the fact that children generally want to please their parents (Robinson & Chase, 2001). The children may have experienced how the acceptance and attention of the parents is dependent on their performance (*ibid.*). Children of workaholics risk learning that they will only win their parents' love if they perform well (Pietropintro, 1986). They consequently become focused on performing in order to gain rewards such as the attention and love of the parents. Diane Fassel, who is, as I mentioned earlier, an expert on the characteristics of workaholics, thinks that this performance-based attention explains why some people develop an addiction to work (Fassel, 1992). The child might be afraid of not getting enough love from its parents if it does not do well in school; consequently, he or she will put all his or her efforts into schoolwork and later into the job (Machlowitz, 1980).

Children of workaholics are often perfectionists, self-critical, and changeable in their behaviour when in the company of adults.

Experts see this as a sign that they strive for recognition (Robinson & Chase, 2001). If the children primarily receive positive attention from their parents when they perform well, this will influence their personalities. This may lead to the perfectionist and competitive sides becoming dominant in the personality of the child. In addition to the positive attention that the child gets from the parents when it makes an effort, the performances may also please the parents. Generally, children want to make their parents happy, so this may be an extra motivation for the child to make an effort. The child is then changing its focus from its own needs in its effort to please its parents. Acting on the basis of others' needs instead of being attentive to your own is, as I mentioned, characteristic of children displaying parentification. Later on in life it may no longer be the parents, but a new "superior", the manager, whom the individual wants to please. And so the efforts to do something extraordinary may last a lifetime.

Work addiction in the next generation

Several studies point to the fact that children of workaholics are themselves caught in the "work-trap" later on in life (Robinson & Chase, 2001). One of these studies shows that the majority of the students who were addicted to work (studying) had parents who were workaholics (Chamberlin, 2001). Furthermore, the study shows that most of the students had different health problems, and suffered from a low degree of physical well-being and low self-acceptance.

What makes these children lose themselves in work? Is it something genetic? We still do not know if it is possible to be genetically predisposed to this kind of addiction. There are, then, no biological, but only psychological, explanations as to why this type of addiction is often carried on in the next generation. Many experts think that the children are copying the behaviour of their parents because the parents are role models to the children (Fassel, 1992). When children whose parents are workaholics develop an addiction, it is not necessarily because they have fond memories of their parents being buried in work. Jonathan, described below, is a good example of this.

Jonathan Lazear, a successful American businessman, became addicted to work just like his father (Lazear, 2001). In his autobiography *The Man Who Mistook his Job for a Life*, he describes his obsession with work. He wonders why he grew up to be like his father, when, as a child, he experienced the negative consequences of work addiction on his own body.

He remembers his father as physically and emotionally absent, because he was always working. When his father worked from home, Jonathan and his brother had to be quiet. His father was often in such a bad mood, caused by his work, that it affected the whole family. They consequently became more sensitive to his state of mind and tried to read his mood in order to find out how to behave. Jonathan and his brother mainly heard their parents talk about their father's job, and, at an early age, they became aware that their father was a very important man and that he commanded respect because of his efforts at work. The father's work consequently took up a lot of space within the family.

Jonathan describes his tense and distanced relationship with his father, and he cannot recall ever wanting to be like his father. Yet, he discovers in adulthood that his life is centred on work, and that his own sons are not as proud of him as he thought they were. On the contrary, they think that he comes across as boasting when he drives around in his expensive cars. Jonathan rethinks his life and begins to give high priority to spending time with his family instead of focusing solely on his career.

It turns out that the parents who are severely addicted to work demand more of their children and their performance than other parents do (Robinson, 1998a). This may be a contributing factor to why these children lose themselves in work, because they have, from an early age, been urged to perform well.

An addiction to work can thus be seen in several generations of the same family. Sometimes, the addiction takes on a new form in the new generation (Robinson, 1998b). One example is children of alcoholics who develop an addiction to work. One explanation as to why this occurs could be the above-mentioned parentification. If the child is prompted to act as an adult and is appreciated for what it *does* rather than for whom it *is*, it may become focused on performance. This creates a foundation for work addiction. In addition, children who grow up in dysfunctional families often find it difficult to determine where their personal responsibility ends (Killinger, 1991). This is caused by, among other reasons, their wanting to satisfy the needs of other family members throughout their childhood. This might also be one of the reasons why these children develop an addiction to work. The risk is there because the child's sense of responsibility makes it difficult for him or her to delegate tasks to others, and they will typically do much more than the job requires of them (*ibid.*).

Children of alcoholics are usually embarrassed on behalf of their family, and in some cases they feel guilty because the grown-up is drinking (Axelrod, 1999; Robinson, 1998a). Furthermore, the children feel as if they are not in control of their own lives, because the behaviour of the alcoholic is typically changeable, which makes the children feel unsafe. The child might feel powerless in relation to his or her family situation, and might therefore start focusing on (school) work, because in this area it may have some control. Good results in school and later at work will necessarily lead to recognition from others, and the child will thus strive to be successful out of fear of ending like the alcoholic parent (Robinson, 1998b).

Bryan Robinson describes in one of his books why he himself got lost in a world of work for many years (Robinson, 1998a). He grew up with an alcoholic father, and, at the age of nine, he took on the responsibility of the home. He was the protector of the family when his father came home drunk, and thus he displayed parentification. When the father did not pick up Bryan and his younger sister as arranged, Bryan tried to act as the adult and calm his sister while they walked home alone through the dark streets. Bryan points out that he did not want this adult role but that he was acting almost instinctively in order to survive.

He began to lose himself in his homework, and spent several hours each day at his desk. As a teenager, he wrote and directed the annual Christmas show, as well as playing the leading role. Bryan explains that, because he did it all by himself and took care of every task, he experienced a sense of control. He experienced a form of stability that he did not get at home. People praised Bryan's hard work and performances, but still he felt inadequate. He started working even harder. This was how the foundation for his work addiction was laid in his teens. The harder he worked at school, and later in his job, the better he felt. Work gave him a sense of control.

Bryan describes how, at the age of forty, he was deeply addicted to work. He would sneak work along on holidays and was constantly thinking of his next project. If he spent a couple of days away from his office he would become irritable and restless, just like his father when he did not get any alcohol. Bryan later acknowledged that he was using work as an escape, so that he would not have to deal with the emotions from his childhood that were still inside him. Today, he is a professor at the University of North Carolina, in addition to counselling clients in his own private practice.

As I have described in this section it can be a crucial factor in one's life if one of your parents was/is addicted to either alcohol or work. Having grown up with either an alcoholic or a workaholic, you have a high risk of becoming a workaholic yourself. The parents, who are a significant part of the environment of our childhood, thus play an important part, but so does the environment of our adult lives. A partner and children form an important part of one's surroundings, and can therefore influence whether or not you get caught up in the "work-trap".

The influence of the family

If, because of your personality, you are predisposed to develop an addiction to work, your partner and any children you might have might be the deciding factors in determining if you do become addicted. The family can be the most important part of your environment in either preventing, triggering, or maintaining the addiction. In this section we examine the conditions within the family that might determine if work takes control of an individual. In Chapter Six, pp. 109–111, I focus on what the family can do to prevent work addiction and help a family member whose life is dominated by work.

What can trigger work addiction?

When an addiction to work is triggered, it might be something within the family that sets it off, such as conflicts in a love relationship. Arguments and disagreements can be emotionally fatiguing, and a way of avoiding these may be to disappear either mentally or physically into one's work. Colleagues do not demand the same level of intimacy as the family does, and relationships at work might therefore be easier to handle and may seem less demanding. Problems in the family might lead an individual unconsciously to choose the "easy" way out, and withdraw completely. The problems, however, will often get worse if the individual chooses to distance himself, and it might therefore often be difficult to determine what is actually causing the problems. Is it because of problems at home that the individual "marries" his job? The adults react to each other's actions and accusations and it becomes difficult to say what started it all (Killinger, 1991; Robinson, 1998a). Typical accusations from the partner may be: "You are never at home, and I am always alone with the children", to which the workaholic might answer, "I would not spend as much time at work if you stopped picking on me" (Robinson, 2001, p. 129). The situation may quickly evolve into a vicious circle in which the work addiction is maintained and the conflict escalates.

If you are predisposed to develop an addiction to work, it is important whether or not your partner distances himself or herself emotionally from you. If your partner withdraws from intimate relations, it might lead you to do the same, and instead focus on the job. In this situation, you might live parallel lives in which you live side-by-side but do not feel any emotional bonds and only rarely do things together. In addition, it may be easier to lose yourself in your work if you feel stressed at home. You might then feel more comfortable at work and may unconsciously strive to spend more time there. As I mentioned in Chapter Two, p. 15 , a study shows that nearly one in five people feel more stress when spending time with their family than they do at work. In addition, one in four feel that they are more in control of time at work than at home (Jensen, 2001). If you experience this kind of difference between work and home, and at the same time have a personality predisposed for addiction, the risk that you will develop an addiction to work is higher than it would be in other people.

It may also be the case that the family admire and praise the workaholic's efforts at work, and this will motivate him to work even harder. Furthermore, if the family tell others of the workaholic's results, he may wish to continue along the same line in order to maintain this admiration from his surroundings. As I described earlier, an addiction to work centres on the one hand on the physical kick, and on the other hand on something psychological in which praise and recognition can be what the individual strives for and becomes addicted to. It is not, therefore, the money that motivates him to work more and indirectly causes the situation. It is actually the pats on the back and the appreciation that comes with a bonus or a pay-rise, as well as the recognition this provides in one's surroundings, which works as the motivation to work harder at the job.

What can maintain an addiction to work?

Different families will react differently to the workaholic's great commitment to the job. The children and the partner will generally try to get the workaholic to participate more in family activities. Some give up if they do not succeed. They may discover that the job is more important to him and that it takes up most of his time. But most families continue the fight, and some even become so focused on changing the workaholic's work habits that it almost becomes an obsession with them. It is more often the partner, rather than the children, who is the most persistent in trying to integrate the workaholic back into the family. But, having a partner who is pressuring you might have the opposite effect, and the workaholic may pull away from the family because he feels that he is not making his own decisions.

In cases of other types of addiction, the partner sometimes acts in a way that maintains the problem. This is also the case of partners of workaholics. The partner may unconsciously support the workaholic's behaviour, resulting in the continuance of the addiction. This "support" may be given in several different ways. The partner may start performing more tasks at home as well as doing any practical work for the workaholic, leaving him more time to spend on the job. The partner may also cover for him, coming up with "white lies" and excuses when he does not keep his commitments to other people because of work. The partner might also arrange family life according to the work habits of the workaholic, so that this does not stand in the way of him working. The following is an example of how a woman arranged her life according to the work addiction of her husband.

Thirty-two-year-old Mary, who had become a mother a couple of months earlier, declined an invitation to her friend's birthday party. She could not attend because she had to stand in for her husband at a christening. Mary's husband was practically always working and was almost never at home. He never participated in family life and if any demands were made on him at home, he would break down and cry. Some of his closest friends had their child christened, but he prioritized work higher and chose not to attend. Mary took on the task and went to the christening, even though she hardly knew his friends. She excused her husband by saying that he was ill. Unfortunately, the christening was held the same day as the birthday party of Mary's friend— to Mary's great regret. Mary and her husband had arranged to talk about their situation and their lives a month and a half later, when things at work were not as hectic.

Mary and other partners in similar situations contribute to maintaining the addiction to work in their partners. Without even knowing it, they are creating the ideal setup for the maintenance and even further development of the behaviour that they are dissatisfied with. In order to help their partner achieve a better balance between the different activities of life, they need to recognize that their own acts are helping to maintain and even worsen the situation. Only after recognizing this can they begin to change the way they act. We may, however, assume that the partner gains something by supporting the addiction, even though he or she does it unconsciously. The question is, what do they gain? It is, of course, impossible to give one answer, as every person is different. It will be particular to each person what the advantage is for him or her. One can imagine how other people will show compassion towards the often difficult situation of the partner, in which he or she alone is responsible for the house and children. This sympathy and care from the surroundings can mean a lot to a person. The partner may also be perceived as having a tremendous amount of energy, and may be admired because he or she takes care of house and children all by himself or herself. Another possibility is that the partner likes to be in the background, carrying the main responsibility for the family, while the hard-working partner is focused on his career. In this way, the partner may not have to get too involved in her own job. It may also be the case that the partner prompts the workaholic to perform well at the job, because a promotion would mean a greater status and more material goods for the family.

The advantages mentioned above are only a selection of those that the partner may experience. No matter what reason people might have for supporting the unhealthy work habits of their partner, they still help maintain the addiction. If the workaholic is to change his life, so that the job takes up less time, the partner needs to stop indirectly supporting the unhealthy patterns. This, however, may only happen if others make the partner aware that what he or she is doing is inappropriate. It is very important that the spouse of a workaholic is made aware of the level of influence and co-responsibility that he or she has.

The influence of the workplace

The technological developments of our society have made several tasks easier as well as faster to perform, both at home and at work. This, however, also means that the pace is a lot faster in several areas of our lives. Because we are *able* to achieve much in a small amount of time, many people feel that they *have to* achieve a lot— both at work and outside. A large number of workplaces are, because of technological development and the global competition among companies, characterized by a fast pace, pressure of time, and large amounts of work burdening the individual employee. Conditions such as these are an ideal basis for an addiction to work to develop, because the set-up makes it possible for a person to work all the time. One part of the environment that can help prevent, trigger, or maintain, an addiction to work is, besides the family, the workplace.

What can trigger and maintain an addiction to work?

One of the conditions that can trigger or maintain an addiction to work is if the workplace is constantly busy and always provides the employee with the opportunity of working overtime. If, in addition, there are no limits to the working hours, or rules concerning counterbalancing overtime, this will, of course, increase the risk that the working hours will be drastically extended. Having the opportunity of working from home might give the employee a better chance of combining work life and private life, but, at the same time, the person may risk losing control of his work habits. In being able to work from home you are at risk of working at all hours of the day, including weekends and holidays, and this can be a pitfall. Many people have explained how, after having worked from home over a period of time, they have reverted to going to the office because they could no longer control their work habits and this started to affect their family life.

A psychologically insecure work environment may also contribute to work taking control of a person (Schaef & Fassel, 1988). If the workplace is characterized by competition and insecurity, it can lead to the individual employee spending a lot of extra time doing his work. This may be the case if the manager, and maybe co-workers as well, look out for mistakes in each others' work. The individual employee will then try to perform his tasks to perfection.

Work addictive companies

The behaviour and attitudes of the manager determine the standards of behaviour in the workplace, because the manager is a role model to his or her employees (Schaef & Fassel, 1988). If the manager is addicted to work, he or she might create a precedent for how many hours you should spend on the job. The manager might also be inclined to appoint people who give as high priority to their jobs as the manager does (Robinson, 1998a). Harry is an example of this.

Thirty-five-year-old Harry explains how, for a couple of years, work came to dominate his entire life. His marriage ended in divorce because his wife did not think that their life would ever change. A couple of years later, Harry started his own consulting firm, where he had to engage people from Sweden. Harry consciously chose to engage people who were as over-committed to their work as he was. He knew that they would be conscientious, and that they would put everything else aside for the job. Harry felt that he knew these people, because he had been like them once. It gave him a sense of comfort, knowing what they stood for.

If managers act like Harry, it will create a majority of workaholics within a company. If the number of employees addicted to work increases, the whole company is at risk of becoming a so-called "addictive organization" (Schaef & Fassel, 1988). This happens when the behaviour patterns of the workaholics become the standard. These patterns include high demands of one's own performance, working for long periods of time, and not being able to delegate tasks to colleagues. If a large number of employees in a company are "married" to their jobs, this may infect other employees with the same tendencies towards work addiction. If a large number of employees stay late at the office, send e-mails at the weekend, or tell others that they work when on holiday, it may create a standard of "this is how we do things around here". This may lead the group of employees to maintain each other in an inappropriate work pattern. The individual employee may thus feel uncommitted or left out if he or she does not share the same standards.

Managers often see it as an asset when employees put a lot of time into the job, and prioritize work above other things. They may even reward those who are most committed to their job, giving them better opportunities for the development of their career, higher pay rises, or simply exempting them from being laid off in times of cutbacks. These employees may then have better opportunities than their colleagues, even though they may not be the best or even the most efficient workers (Jürgensen, 2003). The manager's values consequently play an important part in turning the workplace into a place that triggers and maintains work addiction. (In the next chapter, I describe the consequences it may have for the workplace when an employee is addicted to his work.)

Work and leisure time become one and the same thing

According to Einar Baldursson, who has been working as an occupational health psychologist for twenty-four years, we are not allowing people to distance themselves from their work.

> Employees should be committed to their job and not, as in former times, separate their private and professional lives. The boundaries between leisure time and work time no longer exist. The same is true of the boundaries between our private selves and our professional role. [Rasmussen, 2004b]

This is why, today, we risk being affected personally by conflicts and work-related problems. This happens because the professional role and our private selves have merged into one, caused, among other things, by the breakdown of the boundaries between work and leisure time.

Working on a project basis is a good example of a situation in which leisure time and work overlap. A project is characterized by having a deadline, but no limits on the amount of time spent working on it. You will not have finished the job until the work is done and handed in. The project, then, requires massive results in a short amount of time. During the process you are "on" 100% of the time and you cannot distance yourself from the task. In order to achieve a good result, you need involvement and commitment. It is characteristic of such projects that you work hard and never relax, either mentally or physically, until the job is done. Working on a project basis is gaining ground in a lot of companies. Today, a lot of people are engaged as project managers, or appointed merely to work on a certain project for a specific period of time. The downside might be that the undefined structure of a project allows the employee to let the project dominate his entire life. This may trigger an addiction to work in individuals who have a tendency to let their work control their life.

All in all, there are several circumstances at the workplace that may prevent, trigger, or maintain an addiction to work. The conditions at the company that Steve worked for required the employees to work all the time.

Steve is thirty-six years old and was addicted to work for a long period of time. For several years he sped along, focusing only on his job. But an inspiring book and a wife who said "enough is enough" made him change his life.

"I have always been extremely active and have always filled up my diary as much as possible with different activities. I am 100% devoted to what I am doing, and I have never been one for taking holidays. In my latest job it all fell apart. I had to perform too many tasks in too little time. I would often fall asleep with my laptop on the duvet, and when I awoke I would continue where I had left off. I could only talk about work, and I was never present when I had time off. I would pretend that I was listening to what other people were saying, but my mind was always on the job and the work I had not finished yet. I had no time to be happy and I was always stressed and frustrated. My friends told me that I had changed."

For two and a half years, Steve was the marketing manager of an American company in which most of the employees were workaholics. The company culture supported and maintained the addiction, because there was always an enormous amount of work to be done and impossible deadlines that could never be met. "Everyone was busy and worked at an incredible pace. The manager was constantly sending out conflicting signals when he emphasized that employees had to take care of themselves, but at the same time demanded that deadlines were met. To do both was impossible." Even though Steve worked hard, he could not do all the things he was supposed to do. He chose to work all the time and practically never took any time off. Only by doing this could he avoid a guilty conscience and be happy about himself—because he knew that it would be impossible to work more than he already did. Employees worked more than eighty hours per week and most of them got divorced—including Steve. "It became too much for my wife that I was never at home because of my work. She asked me to resign—which I did. I had read *The Seven Habits of Highly Effective People* (Covey, 1999), a book about the balance between family, work, body, and soul. It helped me to focus on other things besides work. I started my own business, so that, in time, I would be able to work less, but my marriage did not last. Being a self-employed consultant today, I work a lot less than I used to. I am happy and rarely stressed. It is great actually having a life and being able to spend time with my daughter."

Steve has thought a lot about why he was working so much. He thinks it has something to do with recognition. "I tried to live up to something. I wanted to show the world that I *could*. I wanted my father to be proud of me. I sought recognition and got a lot of it at work." Steve feels that the work addiction is still in him. He knows that it requires a conscious effort to maintain his new lifestyle. "My father worked all the time, so I didn't get it from strangers. I have to be careful not to get caught again. I have written down some 'rules' to remind me about the balance between body and soul. And, luckily, my friends look out for me." Steve continues, "If you want to break out of work addiction, the most important thing is to figure out the reason why you work so much. In addition, you have to pay close attention to the kind of culture that exists at the company in which you work. If it is an unhealthy culture, in which many employees are addicted to work, it is better to find another job, so that the company does not keep you trapped in some bad work habits."

Culture and society

Standards and values

In understanding what may influence the development and the maintaining of an addiction to work, it is necessary also to include culture and society, as they form our overall environment. Culture and society also play an important part in determining if some individuals will become addicted to work.

There are several conditions within western culture that may promote the risk of a work addiction being triggered in a person predisposed to addiction. It is an overall question of the standards and values that are anchored in our culture. Our society is built on values, Christian values, in which hard work is seen as a virtue. In addition, today we see prestige as connected to being busy and building a career. It is seen as a valuable asset to be able to work hard. Our society, the "information society" as we call it, requires a whole new type of employee. The modern employee is supposed to be able to work at all hours and anywhere, and thus be 100% flexible (Stenstrup, 1998). Demands such as these will inevitably increase the risk that an addiction to work is developed and/or maintained.

The influence of the media

The media in a society plays an important part in relation to public opinion, and is consequently an important part of the overall environment. The media influences our attitudes towards work. When they take up stories about "super-people", who lead interesting lives, have an exciting career, are able to overcome incredible things, and at the same time work long hours every week, they make role models of these people, which we then strive to be like. Advertisements, trying to prompt us to consume more, may also indirectly speed up the pace at work and make us focus even more on the job.

Different societies' attitudes to work

Work has different meanings and different values in different societies. In several countries around the world, work is treated with contempt and is mainly something performed by women. In some places they try to work as little as possible, and in some cases the people who work are looked down upon. The rich have other people to work for them, and they spend their time on amusements. Because of cultural differences, it is therefore difficult to imagine that the same number of people would devote their lives to work in an African country as in the countries of Northern Europe. Our recognition of hard work and admiration for those who are busy and work long hours may indirectly be the cause of some people being workaholics. Our standards and values in Northern Europe, and in Northern America, thus influence what people may lose themselves in.

In different cultures, there will be different definitions of when something is too much. In Japan, where they have a tradition for working long hours, they will, of course, have different standards for when work takes up so much time in your life that it becomes a problem. It is, therefore, important what cultural context you live in. Culture and society are part of the environment, and may be contributing factors in a person developing or maintaining an addiction to work.

CHAPTER FIVE

What happens when work takes control?

'Work seven days a week and nothing can stop you'

(John Moore)

I t can be very satisfying to be committed to a job you find interesting and which offers you experiences and challenges that
suit your personality and qualifications. However, if the job has
taken control and has started to dominate your life, it may lead to
a series of serious consequences, for yourself, your family, and your
colleagues. In some cases, though, it may be difficult to establish
whether the problems are the result of your commitment to the job.
Several studies show that certain problems and difficulties occur *at
the same time* as an addiction to work. In this chapter, I present the
difficulties and costs that are the result of, or are related to, an
addiction to work.

Going back in time 100 years, or even merely fifty years, the
working conditions were, in many ways, much poorer than they are
today. In particular, the physical settings have become much health-
ier today than they were in previous times. In addition, many
people today have a say in the planning and execution of their own

jobs. Being able to control one's own workday is seen by many employees as a liberation when compared with the old days when employees were "trapped" in time and space. It is, without a doubt, an advantage to feel liberated in one's job, but the more liberated the workplace is, the harder it becomes to liberate oneself from it. For example, working from home provides the employee with a large amount of freedom, as he or she is able to decide for him/herself when to work. But when work is suddenly part of one's home it will impose on one's private sphere. This means that it becomes difficult to let go of the work and take time off. If the job starts taking up more and more of a person's time, he may not even realize it himself because it happens gradually. If it takes control he becomes trapped in a vicious circle that is difficult to break out of. The addiction may be allowed to develop further because many people still do not recognize work addiction for what it is. The more severe the addiction is the greater will be the consequences for the individual and his surroundings.

The workaholic's problems

Loss of contact with self and others

If your life consists of nothing but work, it becomes easy to live solely for the job, and life is at risk of becoming very serious because playing, spontaneity, and time to just "be" will be put aside or forgotten. If you want to be a "whole" person, you have to use yourself in different ways. Human beings are multi-faceted and life offers a variety of great and different experiences. The only thing we need to do is to recognize these possibilities and to choose to try them out. If you want to evolve, you need to do something different from what you normally do; this is true of many different areas of life. Luckily, there are many jobs that challenge us and give us the opportunity to develop both personally and professionally. It may, however, be dangerous to rely solely on one's job to fulfil one's needs. Being "married" to the job, you will often be blind to the many opportunities outside the workplace. You risk finding yourself in a world of work, and, in the worst scenario, you become cut off from your family, as well as from yourself and your emotions

(Lazear, 2001). Those severely addicted to their jobs are rarely in touch with their emotions and might, as a consequence, have no sense of how they really feel. Being constantly occupied by something (work) both physically and mentally, you are at risk of losing touch with your feeling and your needs. This happens because you are always focusing on something external—work—instead of focusing on your emotions.

> Sarah is married to a man who works ninety hours a week. He has always spent a lot of time at work, but over the past five years it has become worse. She explains how he is now living in isolation from her and their three-year-old son. He has lost contact with his feelings, and says that he does not care about anything. Things that would previously have made him sad no longer affect him. For example, he left his most treasured item, a watch which was an heirloom, on a bench—and it was gone when he returned. He was sad for about five minutes, but rushed along and soon forgot about the incident.

> Sarah explains how he keeps aiming higher and higher, and the only thing he can think about is the next job. She often finds her husband sleeping at the desk in his home office. When she wakes him up he exclaims, "I have to work, I mustn't sleep." The ulcer that he developed some years ago has started bothering him again, and so has his psoriasis. Sarah thinks that he is aware that he is working too much. The problem, however, is that he is unable to limit how much space the job should be allowed to take in his life. He does not know how to regain control of his life.

A one-sided life

In addition to the problems mentioned earlier of drifting into a world of work, there are other consequences of occupying oneself solely with one's job. One such consequence is that you are at risk of leading a very one-sided life. To build your life around one single activity (work) is dangerous, as you risk losing everything if you are laid off or when you retire. It is commonly acknowledged that people whose life has been centred solely on their job often experience a personal crisis when they are laid off or retire. They often have no interests or hobbies outside work, because all their time and energy has been concentrated on their job. Therefore, they have nothing in their lives that may compensate for the loss of their job.

Being devoted to the job also makes you more vulnerable to defeats in the workplace. If you make mistakes, or do not perform as well as expected, you may easily be "knocked back" and feel stupid and incompetent unless other areas of your life give you confidence and meaning. The more areas of life that give you plea-sure, and maybe even make you feel competent, the easier it will be for you to handle crises in other areas of life. It is therefore inap-propriate to found your whole life around the job.

Friends disappear

Another problem related to work addiction is the gradual loss of friends (Lazear, 2001). This happens because the workaholic spends most of his time at work, which is his top priority. Another reason why the workaholic's friends often disappear is that in most cases he makes new friends in the workplace. To all of us, socializing with colleagues can develop into more or less close-knit relationships, and this may be an advantage. It is nice to go to work if there are people there with whom we feel comfortable and like talking to. One disadvantage, however, is that you risk losing your colleague friends if you lose your job. Unless it is a stable and strong friend-ship, in which both parties are willing to invest time when they are not at work, it may easily dissolve when you do not automatically meet in the workplace.

Having social relations and friendships outside the job will give you strength in case of a change of jobs or if you lose the one you have. The social support of family, friends, and acquaintances are of great value to us humans and help us get through though situations in life. In the previously mentioned book, *The Man Who Mistook his Job for a Life*, Jonathan Lazear (*ibid.*) describes his own addiction to work. He mentions how one consequence is that the workaholic isolates himself in his job. He sets aside family and friends, result-ing in him becoming lonely. Lazear points to the fact that the workaholic is close to no one—not even himself.

Health is ignored

If you prioritize work above all other things you will often neglect other considerations, such as taking care of yourself and your health. There are numerous examples of people severely addicted to their work who, despite warning signals from their body, have not slowed down at work (Chamberlin, 2001; Danish Radio Documentry, 2002).

> David Adams, who was the managing director of a large advertising company, is only one of such examples (Jürgensen, 2003). Shortly before his thirty-seventh birthday, he started developing tics around the eyes, had difficulty speaking, and found it hard to concentrate. Things were swimming before his eyes and his physician had him picked up by an ambulance. He found it difficult to lift his legs and could not walk in a straight line. The doctors assessed David's condition to be life-threatening, due either to a brain tumour or a stroke. It later turned out that the problems were caused by stress. Over a long period of time David had been working too many hours and too hard. After the stay at the hospital he denied that the situation was caused by too much work. He has later come to realize that he was addicted to work. Today, David has changed his life. He spends more time at home, has taken up fishing, and has started working less. Life is too precious, he thinks, for him to want to die because of a job.

When leisure time is limited because of work, sports and other forms of physical activities, which were formerly a part of one's life, are often reduced or completely dropped. Investing in one's health by spending time on keeping in shape and exercising, not only increase your physical wellbeing it also reduces stress, prevents illness and other physical problems. It is therefore worrying when these kinds of activities are put aside because of work. Many people who are addicted to work suffer from health problems and a majority of them suffer from stress (Bonebright, Clay, & Ankermann, 2000).

Stress

Another problem related to work addiction is stress. Studies show that people who have lost control of their work habits suffer from job-related stress more often than other people (*ibid.*). It is, therefore, relevant to deal with stress in relation to work addiction. It is, however, important to emphasize that even though workaholics often suffer from stress, it does not mean that people who are stressed are also workaholics. It is possible to be stressed for a period of time—long or short—without having lost control of one's work habits. Thus, stress and work addiction are two different problems that sometimes appear at the same time in the same person.

In the following section I define what stress is and what leads to stress. How to prevent and fight stress and work addiction is discussed in Chapter Six. If you wish to know more about stress, I would refer you to the many books on the subject.

What is stress?

We talk a lot about stress and the media pay a lot of attention to the phenomenon. Stress is often confused with being busy and with different kinds of physical and mental problems this causes some confusion about the definition of the term. Stress is a complex phenomenon and experts cannot agree on a single definition. Some emphasize the physical aspects, while others emphasize the mental aspects when trying to understand what stress is.

In the course of this book, I base my view of stress on that of Bo Netterstrøm, a consultant doctor with twenty-five years' specialization in stress. He defines stress as: "A condition in the organism which is physiologically characterized by a release of energy, and psychologically by dislike and tension" (Netterstrøm, 2002). Stress is consequently not an *illness* but a *condition*, which nevertheless has to be taken seriously because it can lead to different illnesses. Being exposed to a great strain, or being stressed over a long period of time, may result in an illness, which, in the worst cases, may lead to death.

Stress will usually appear gradually, and therefore we grow accustomed to being stressed. The unpleasant state becomes normal, which leads some people to become even more stressed and to do nothing about it. The frog in the pot is a good example of what happens. It is said that a frog will jump out of the water if you put it into a pot of boiling water. If you heat up the water slowly, while the frog is in the pot, however, it will eventually boil to death. This happens because the frog gradually becomes accustomed to the situation and as a consequence does not react to it. The same can happen to people. Often we will not react to the uncomfortable situation of stress, but will stay in it and become even more stressed. This happens because most people will not admit that they are stressed. Many people think that it is embarrassing to be stressed and see it as a sign of weakness, and consequently they do not want others to know. Colleagues and the manager are often the last people to whom an individual wants to disclose this. The stressed individual constantly hopes that the unpleasantness will stop. "After the deadline next Thursday, everything will be better", or "Management will soon hire more people and then I will have less to do", are the thoughts and statements with which the stressed person stalls him/herself.

Physiological changes

If we are to make an extra effort, such as working hard, the first thing that happens is that our body prepares itself for the physical challenge. It is practical and stimulating that the body is put on high alert when it comes to stress. Within the body, the levels of the stress hormones noradrenalin, adrenalin, and cortisol are increased. The release of noradrenalin and adrenalin leads to an increase in the number of heartbeats, a rise in the blood pressure, and the blood vessels are contracted in certain areas while they are expanded in others. Cortisol stimulates the immune system into fighting off infections. However, if the cortisol levels are high during a long period of time, it has the opposite effect, as the immune system will then be weakened and its ability to fight off disease will decrease. In addition to the stress hormones, the hypothalamus will release endorphins, which function as natural pain-killers. Sugar will be released into the bloodstream, resulting in a short-lived energy boost. Breathing will become faster, sending larger amounts of oxygen and nutrients to muscles and lungs via the blood. Finally, you will sweat more, in order to cool down the overheated body.

All of these physiological reactions help us when we need to do something out of the ordinary; they also help us when we are in physically and mentally challenging situations. If we are often stressed, the body will not have the required time to restore our health. It will be worn out and vulnerable in future situations of stress. If we find ourselves in a state of stress over a long period of time, these reactions become hazardous to our health. Prolonged stress may, among other things, lead to depression, hardening of the arteries, and strokes. Stress may also worsen any illnesses you already suffer from, such as pains and aches as well as asthma and allergies, among others (Friström, 2003; Grunnet, 1989).

How many people feel stressed?

The number of people who, for a period, are unable to work because of stress is increasing. There are also indications that many more people suffer from stress than is indicated in some statistics. A primary reason for this is that the symptoms of stress are often mistaken for other illnesses. Another reason is that talking about stress is taboo, and many people find it embarrassing to be unable to cope with their job. This is why it often takes a long time for people to seek help. In addition, many employees today are extremely conscientious. They know that their colleagues will have more work to do if they call in sick, and as a consequence they over-burden themselves (Sørensen, 2004).

In a European study of the working conditions in fifteen EU countries, the responses were:

• 28% said yes to suffering from work-related stress on a daily basis;
• 23% said yes to suffering from work-related fatigue.

A Danish study shows that the number of people suffering from work-related stress and fatigue are slightly fewer than in the European study. The numbers from the Danish study indicate that somewhere between one in four and one in five workers are stressed on a daily basis, but the conditions vary greatly according to profession (Netterstrøm, 2002).

Many Danes say that they feel pressured in their daily lives. This is supported by a study conducted by Gallup for *Ugebrevet A4* (a weekly newsletter published by the Danish Trades Union Congress), in which 75% of the Danes answered that they would like to lead less busy lives (Danish Radio News, 2004). This high number does not indicate that all these people feel stressed; it is, however, alarming, because it shows that three out of four Danes are too busy.

Stressors

The conditions that stress us are called stressors, and they can come in many different shapes. Stressors are divided into three groups: life events, physical stressors, and psychological stressors. How much the individual stressor will influence us depends on what we think about them, meaning whether we perceive them as positive or negative.

Life events are seen as stressors because they carry with them great changes in our lives. A serious illness, the death of a close relative, divorce, or the loss of one's job are all examples of events that may lead a person to become stressed. Also marriage, pregnancy, and a voluntary change of jobs can cause stress, even though these are seen as happy events. If several great changes take place within a short period of time, there is a higher risk of you becoming stressed. Our reactions to these events, however, are very different. A death in the family might, for some people, be a relief if the person who dies had been ill for a long time, whereas for other people it may be a great weight to carry. Getting married, to some people, is a rather unproblematic affair, whereas others may worry about the future. How we are affected by changes in our life is very much dependent on who we are and how we perceive these changes.

Physical stressors can be things such as noise, pollution, or cold. We are all affected by the physical conditions around us, but whether one feels bothered about it differs from person to person. This is related to whether you are affected *psychologically* or not. The physical stressors are concrete and can be measured. They are, therefore, easier to relate to and to change than the psychological stressors, which are much more diffuse.

Psychological stressors are problems and conflicts either at home or at the workplace. They can be disagreements and arguments with the partner or other family members, financial difficulties, illness, problems relating to a change of home, or a career change. Mental stressors can also be arguments with colleagues or the manager, a lack of influence at work, or the fact that you are too busy and overburdened, all of which makes going to work seem almost impossible. How much we are stressed by these things is also dependent on what we think about them. The psychological stressors are intangible, and can therefore be hard to handle and to change. Many people underestimate the effect of these stressors, but conflicts and problems can cause a great deal of strain. You should, therefore, look out for any signs of stress if these psychological stressors are present in your life (Milsted, 1999).

Symptoms

We all react differently to stress. Some people develop stomach-aches, some become irritable and start to snap at their partner, others have difficulty falling asleep at night, and still others have a constant cold. It can be a great help to know the symptoms of stress and your own reactions to them. Stress shows itself through physical, psychological, or behavioural signs. The physical symptoms are often mistaken for illness, and many people therefore assume that the uncomfortable state has a biological cause. The psychological and behavioural symptoms are often belittled, and thought to be caused by things other than stress. "I don't eat that much these days, but let's not make a big deal of that", or "I have been feeling tired for some time now, but it will probably soon go away" are sentences that exemplify such belittlements. Table 3 provides a guide to the symptoms of stress.

The symptoms listed in Table 3 are mentioned at random (Grunnet, 1989; Hauschlidt, 2004; Milsted, 1999). It is impossible to say how many of the symptoms have to be present for a person to be stressed. If you display as few as one or two of the danger signals it is a good idea to stop and ask yourself if you suffer from stress. Then you might try to change the situation or the way you think about the situation. It may be difficult to see if you have changed because of stress, so it might be a good idea to seek the help of the people closest to you. Colleagues and family might, for example, tell you if you are displaying signs of stress. Being stressed for only a short period of time, however, should not cause you any concern.

Mental consequences

In addition to the symptoms described above, which in themselves can be unpleasant and reduce your quality of life, there are also

Table 3.   The signs and symptoms of stress.

The physical symptoms	The psychological and behavioural symptoms
Palpitation	Irritability
Dizziness	Restlessness
Headaches	Unrest
Indigestion	Concentration difficulties
Shortness of breath	Slips of the memory
Abdominal pains	Sadness
Aching muscles	No sense of humour
Diarrhoea	Anxiety
Shaking	Lack of passion and energy
Tics	Exhaustion
Constant colds	Insecurity
Hypersensitivity to noises or smells	Sleep deprivation
Lack of sexual drive	Being absent due to illness
Changes in weight	A tendency to isolate oneself
Heartburn	Fits of rage
Nausea	Increasing use of stimulants such as caffeine, alcohol, or tobacco
Chest pains	Being unable to relax
Fatigue	Indecisiveness
Worsening of asthma or allergies	

mental inconveniences that come with being stressed for a long period of time. One example is that people who are stressed often have difficulty learning new things. Their attention span is weakened, and their time of reaction has decreased. Thus, they are able to "contain" less mentally than they did before, and as a consequence they work slower. People who are stressed might also find it difficult to make rational decisions, because they are unable to keep a broad view of things. This means that people who are stressed often make more mistakes than other people. In addition, you also lose your sense of time when you are stressed, and as a consequence you always feel that you are behind with your work. All in all, the quality of your work deteriorates when you are stressed, and your performance at work is reduced. Long-term stress may also impair your empathy and lead to a state of mental exhaustion or depression (Baldursson, 2002).

Karoshi

The most serious consequence of stress is death. A new phenomenon called *karoshi*, which means to die from over-exertion in
connection with one's job, has seen the light of day. Several
instances have already been recorded in Japan, which for many
years has been known for a strict work culture including long work
hours and short holidays. It is customary in many Japanese busi-
nesses for the employees to work 10–12 hours every day. One of the
side effects of this great work effort is that some people suddenly
die from over-exertion at work. In recent years an increasing number of Japanese men are dying because of too much work pressure.
The majority of these men are in their forties and fifties. Studies
have shown that the *karoshi* deaths are caused by stress, which is
caused by too great a workload over a long period of time. The
specific cause of death is, in most cases, thought to be disturbances
in the heart rhythm (Ishiyama & Katayama, 1994). Japan has, for a
long time, had the world's lowest mortality rate when it comes to
heart disease, but this record is now challenged by the strict work
culture and the high level of stress in the population. If we do not
work to prevent and to battle stress more efficiently than we do
now, we may soon see the *karoshi* phenomenon coming to Western
Europe. In Sweden, they have already recorded two instances of
karoshi (Rajs, Perski, Blomqvist, Hammerstrom, & Hammerstrom,
2001).

Burn-out

One of the most serious side effects of work addiction is burn-out.
Studies have shown that if you put in a great effort at work and at
the same time feel stressed, it may lead to you becoming burnt out
(Bonebright, Clay, & Ankermann, 2000). Burn-out develops over a
long period of time and many people do not see what is happening
until one day they wake up unable to get out of bed. They do not
feel like going to work, and may feel completely devoid of energy
and motivation. Many people who are overly involved in their
work experience burn-out, and it is often at this point that they realize they need to change their work habits and their relationship to
their work (Robinson, 1998). (See for example the story of Henrik

Graversen, pp. 21–22.) A number of these people are so worn out that they are referred to a clinic specializing in occupational health for an examination. Others seek the help of psychologists on their own.

Burn-out is an ongoing process in which a devoted employee gradually loses his or her motivation and enjoyment of the job due to work-related stress. Burn-out is described as *a syndrome of emotional exhaustion, depersonalization, and reduced personal accomplishment that can occur among individuals who do "people work" of some kind* (Maslach, Jackson, & Leiter, 1996). The person who is burnt out may experience a change of personality that is characterized by negative attitudes towards other people. In addition, the level of performance as well as the efficiency of the individual will drop. The person will often be unaware that he or she is changing, because the changes happen gradually and over a long period of time. One of the early signs of burn-out is when the person can no longer find any purpose in his or her work.

The key aspects of burn-out syndrome are the following:

Emotional exhaustion: a feeling of having no energy and being unable to give anything of oneself psychologically.

Depersonalization: negative, cynical attitudes and feelings about one's clients.

Reduced personal accomplishments: a tendency to evaluate oneself negatively, particularly with regard to one's work with clients (Maslach, Jackson, & Leiter, 1996).

Causes of burn-out

Burn-out was first discovered in social workers whose jobs demand a great human commitment (Graversgaard, 1994). People who work in jobs that require close personal contact with clients, such as pedagogical work, nursing, and police work are at high risk of burning out. What is characteristic of these "service professions" is that they demand great empathy and it can be extremely demanding to work like this. The risk of burn-out is even higher when the individual makes great demands on him/herself and the job. The more an employee gets involved personally and emotionally in the job the higher is the risk of burn-out. In many jobs today, companies expect a great commitment from the employee at the same time as they make great demands of him or her and expect a fast work pace. This, without a doubt, contributes to an increased risk of burn-out (*ibid.*).

Burn-out also occurs when the individual's values and ambitions collide with the realities of the workplace. Many organizations do not live up to their own goals, and this may disappoint and disillusion the employees. A contributing factor to burn-out, then, is a discrepancy between the goals and the ethos of the workplace. Many people experience that rules and procedures stand in the way of them doing their job properly; this, too, can lead to burn-out. Within organizations in which the role of the individual employee is unclear, and in which the requirements of the job are in conflict, employees have a higher risk of burning out (*ibid*).

A typical process of burn-out goes through the following five phases:

1. Ambivalence and doubt
2. Frustration and feeling powerless
3. Giving up and resignation
4. Cynicism and apathy
5. Burn-out (*ibid.*)

There may be several reasons why some people burn out. The most important are: overtaxing, lack of self-determination, and autonomy, as well as lack of rewards and human resource management (*ibid.*).

Overtaxing can be divided into three forms:

Objective overtaxing: the workload is unrealistically heavy.
Subjective overtaxing: the workload is felt as being too heavy or the job is perceived to be hard and fatiguing.
Qualitative overtaxing: the job requires skills and qualifications that the employee does not possess.

Lack of self-determination and autonomy is when changes are not communicated to the employee, or when the individual has no influence on his own work hours or how the job is to be performed. This may lead to a negative attitude towards management and the job.

Lack of rewards and human resource management is when management does not recognize and appreciate an employee or group of employees, their effort and performance at the job. Human resource management is something the organization has to put on the agenda and accord high priority. This may take different forms, such as company events or trips that strengthen community feeling and show that the company recognizes the efforts of the employees by spending money on them.

The responsibility of management

The three causes of burn-out mentioned above are largely the responsibility of the management. Earlier, it was assumed that burn-out was an individual problem, but the causes reveal that certain conditions in the workplace, over which the individual has no control, are important in the process of burn-out. It is, therefore, important that the workplace sets up some limits that may help to prevent burn-out in employees. For this to work, a healthy company culture is necessary. The managers might, for example, appear as role models for how you prevent yourself from burning out. This may happen through managers and employees having realistic expectations as to which goals can be achieved in the job, and by not taking it personally and blaming themselves when things do not succeed. This is best achieved by not identifying too strongly with one's job title, but instead anchoring oneself in other roles in one's life, such as the role of mother, partner, or sportsman. The Florence Nightingale syndrome, in which one's job becomes one's calling, is dangerous because it leads to a merger of one's professional role and one's private self. When this merger occurs, the private self will see it as a defeat if and when the professional self is not successful.

Below is an example of a workaholic who experienced burn-out.

Thirty-six-year-old Laura was addicted to work for several years. She is trained in the advertising business and made a career for herself in America, where she worked eighty hours per week, until she burnt out. Today she gives talks about her experiences of burn-out. She thinks that it is important that her message comes across so that others may prevent themselves from going through what she went through. Laura explains how she has had work addiction in her for as long as she can remember. As a child, it was not work that she was addicted to but rather a wish to perform and to prove to herself and others that she could do it. Her father and she had a relationship characterized by competitions. She wanted to show him that she was good.

Laura sees the same tendency in many of the women she meets. "They do not want to disappoint their boss, so they do not tell him 'no' when, for the third time that day, he piles a large stack of tasks on their desk. They demand great things of themselves and want to be perfect and show the world how good they are. This is why they take on more and more tasks." Laura thinks that these women are screaming for affirmation—they want to be seen and to be recognized. Laura is, therefore, very alert to her colleagues starting to overburden themselves. Laura knows that people do not see it themselves if they are on the road to burn-out. This is why it is important that others help you, before it is too late.

Laura did not know that she was addicted to work. Both her husband and she worked a lot. They were both successful in their jobs and worked their way up through the hierarchy. Everyone in the company was very committed to their job, so Laura and her husband were not the only ones who stayed at the office till 11 p.m. They never took time off, as there were always new projects to be discussed and developed. They even worked on Christmas Eve and New Year's Eve. Laura was always pursuing new goals, she was always moving on, and she did everything 120%.

"When I had my daughter, I took only six weeks maternity leave. I saw Sophie as a new client and read everything about children. She cried a lot the first year. I would walk around with her at night, while I was writing down new ideas for work on pieces of paper scattered around the house. I felt that I had to make the most of the time. It was a tough year. I almost never got any sleep." Laura went to the doctor because of respiratory problems. The doctor thought that she might be suffering from stress, and that she was overburdening herself. She denied that. Her family, too, was worried, and they tried to get her to slow down, without any luck. "I didn't listen to them because I didn't think that I had a problem. According to my own definition I was a success: I made a lot of money, I had an impressive job title, a great responsibility, and several subordinates."

It was at a birthday party that the young career-woman realized that work took up too much time. "The man next to me asked me what I did in my spare time. I proudly answered that I worked. He asked again and I explained that I had no spare time, because I was always working. He looked at me in a funny way and turned round to talk to the woman on his other side. I felt very uninteresting."

Late that night when Laura got home, she bought a dog on the Internet, not because she wanted a dog, but now at least her husband and she could *say* that they had a hobby. It later turned out that the dog changed their lives and helped save them from the addiction. "We went to pick up the dog, and suddenly we sat there in the kennel and looked at the little fellow for an hour. For the first time in many years we did not think about work. It was wonderful. Even though we cheated a bit in the beginning and paid somebody to walk the dog in the evening so that we did not have to come home early, it still meant something. After a while we started coming home early and we realized how relaxing it was to play with the dog."

The burn-out came just as Laura achieved her ultimate goal: being appointed MD of the advertising agency she was working for. She declined the offer and resigned. At that time she had no energy and cared about nothing. "I felt a sense of emptiness and only looked forward to finishing projects and other tasks instead of enjoying doing my job, as I used to. I had no energy, I was very impatient, and was often in a bad mood. Before I had focused on climbing up within the company, but that had changed too." The family wanted a better balance in their life and returned to Denmark, where both Laura and her husband were born and raised. Laura did not realize that she was burnt-out and, as a consequence, she did not seek any help. "It took a very long time before I realized that what I experienced was burn-out, and it took several years to get over it. I also had a couple of relapses along the way. It would have been much better if I had had help from the beginning."

Today, Laura works thirty-seven hours per week and works from home one day a week. She enjoys the limited work hours, which leaves her time to spend with her daughter and the dog. She is very aware of any signals from her body. She can stop herself when she feels she is getting stressed by going to the toilet to meditate. "When I started meditating, it didn't work at all. I almost became aggressive, because I felt completely unproductive just sitting there doing nothing." But her will-power succeeded, and after months of practice she managed to learn it. She is also much better at limiting herself and saying no.

The tendency to return to the old pattern of work addiction will always be present, so Laura knows that in the future she will have to be very attentive to her work habits. Her ambition is to live in the now and to balance her work life and private life. "I don't want ever again to be a workaholic. It was a clear case of addiction; I needed my 'drug' in order to achieve a happy feeling. Of course, it is great to be constantly 'high' and have a lot of energy, but besides that there is nothing positive about work addiction. You feel as if you live in another world, and you don't give high priority to family and friends because you don't understand what really matters in life."

Laura thinks that it is important to prevent workaholism, and to start educating as early as primary school about the risks people run if they focus only on work and career. When you have become a workaholic you rarely listen to advice from others, so something drastic has to happen, such as a divorce or burn-out, before you make any changes in your life.

The family

A sense of betrayal

As I have mentioned earlier, workaholics find it difficult to let go of their work and to relax. As a consequence, holidays can be something of a challenge. If you are severely addicted to your work, you will typically avoid going on holiday, or may bring work along so that it is no longer a holiday.

> A forty-year-old self-employed man had cancelled two separate holidays with his family—because of his work—within the past seven months. He was a bit worried about the situation, but ensured that the Christmas holiday, a couple of months away, would definitely not be cancelled.

Many adults call the time they spend with their families "quality time". This term signifies that the amount of time is limited, but that the content in return is very valuable. "Quality time" is free from stress and arguments and is characterized by people being mentally present and enjoying themselves together. In some cases, it almost sounds as if the term is used to justify not spending enough time with one's partner and children. If you spend most of your energy and waking hours at work, you will naturally have less time and energy for other parts of your life, including your family.

Even if you are not a workaholic *per se*, but just work a lot, it may have consequences for your family—consequences to do with absence. If you have a partner or children, it is naturally important to them if you are present or not. They would, in most cases, rather spend twenty-five hours with you as opposed to only two, if they could choose. In many cases, family members want to spend more time with the person who is working a lot. Many family members miss the person and even feel betrayed (Fassel 1992). They might feel betrayed in different ways. In everyday life, the workaholic might come home later than he had promised and dinner with the family is either postponed or missed. Vacations or arrangements to spend time together during holidays may be cancelled because of work. Birthdays and other family events may also be given low priority. The family might, in these cases, feel betrayed, and be left with a feeling that they do not matter at all to the person (*ibid.*). In the worst cases, they lose confidence in the workaholic because he does not keep his promises. Broken promises may cause a lack of trust that can be hard to mend.

Jack, a thirty-six-year-old Canadian, is married to Susan, with whom he shares an apartment. The couple has three little boys, whom Susan looks after at home. Jack, who is a chef, is in the middle of making a career in the restaurant business, this means long days at work and working at the weekends. It is a silent agreement between them that Susan is in charge of the home and children. At one point Jack is offered a two-week trip to Spain to work, but Susan thinks that it is too long for her to stay home alone with the boys. They reach a settlement and agree that he can go for a week.

When the week has passed, Jack phones Susan to change the arrangement so that he can stay a week longer. The restaurant needs him and he wants to continue his work. Jack's wife maintains that the arrangement was only for a week and refuses to allow him to stay in Spain. The Canadian chef has to confess that, despite their arrangement, he promised his employer to stay for two weeks. Susan is very frustrated; she feels powerless and tells her friends about the incident.

When she first met Jack he was very committed to his work. She thought that it was a positive sign that he was ambitious, but she also thought that his zeal would decrease when they had children. Jack, however, does not hide the fact that work is still the most important thing in his life. He actually tells his friends and his wife, "My work is my life—I have nothing else!" Susan is unhappy with his statements, but she feels that there is nothing she can do about it.

Mentally absent from the family

One way of avoiding being absent from the family for too long is, if possible, to set up a workplace at home. One of the advantages of this is that you are both at home and at work at the same time. In addition, you do not have to worry about any time spent on transportation to and from work. One of the disadvantages for the family, however, is the paradox of being physically present but not being able to participate actively in family life because you are at work. You are physically present, but mentally absent. "I am working and I do not want to be disturbed" is often said, directly or indirectly. Another situation that is characterized by physical presence and mental absence is when you come home tired after a long hard day at work. The lack of energy that is caused by being tired might make it difficult for you to concentrate and to be emotionally present. This is probably something we have all experienced. Other instances in which we are mentally absent are when we are not at work but our minds are still focused on the job, and, as a consequence, we are not paying attention to where we are. This is also something that most of us have experienced.

Partners of people who work a lot have told me that the mental absence is often more difficult to handle and accept than the physical (Robinson, 1998). If the person is not at home, it is easy to deal with the situation because it is concrete. If the person is at home, however, the partner will naturally expect emotional and physical contact that is not there because the person is mentally absent. It can be very frustrating to experience the paradox of a person who is there without being present. What is the use of him being in the room if he cannot be reached mentally?

The ambivalent feelings of the family

Family members are often unhappy about not spending enough time with the workaholic (Fassel, 1992, Machlowitz, 1980). The different emotions they have in relation to this, as well as any resentment they might feel because they are not put before the job, are feelings that the families often find hard to allow themselves to have (Fassel, 1992). This is probably due to the fact that focusing on one's career and working hard is prestigious and greatly valued in our culture. Friends and neighbours of the family might be impressed that the person is able to cope with so much work. It might therefore be difficult for the family to be unhappy about something that is praised and admired by others. In addition, the family might also benefit from the material goods that are often the rewards of a person working hard. Moreover, if the person tells his family that he is sacrificing himself for their sake, and works hard so that they are able to buy many things, it might be difficult for the family to be unhappy about it (Robinson, 1989). This is why, in many cases, the negative feelings of the children and the partner are followed by feelings of guilt. They may feel guilty for feeling unhappy about something for which they think they ought to be thankful.

If we compare the families of workaholics with those of alcoholics, we find that it is easier for the family of the alcoholic to relate to the problem and consequently to place their anger (Robinson & Chase, 2001). The alcohol and the bottles are the "bad guys" in their minds. These are something concrete, and, as a consequence, the addiction might be easier to relate to. In the family of the workaholic, the problem, however, is invisible and diffuse.

The partner's experience of the marriage

In the USA, several studies have been conducted as to what it is like to be married to a person severely addicted to his or her work (Robinson, 1998; Robinson, Carroll, & Flowers, 2001). In a study from 1998, 326 randomly chosen married women were divided into two groups (Robinson & Kelly, 1998). One group consisted of women who were married to workaholics (defined on the basis of the test on p. 43), while the other group consisted of women whose husbands were not addicted to work. The study showed that the women who were married to workaholics experienced a larger degree of marital alienation, had fewer positive feelings towards their husbands, as well as a greater degree of external locus of control. External locus of control is when an individual feels as if he or she has no influence on his or her own life. You feel as if you have no control of things that happen in your life, and that events are more often caused by other people, luck, or faith. The study indicates that these women generally feel that they have no influence over their own lives. They probably do not think that they are in charge of their own lives. This external locus of control might thus be the reason why these women stay with their workaholic husbands even though they feel alienated in their marriage and have fewer positive feelings towards their husbands than the other group of women had.

In accordance with this, a questionnaire-study showed that wives of workaholics are a lot less caring towards their husbands in relation to women married to non-addicts (Carroll & Robinson, 2000). In addition, the wives of workaholics do not feel as connected to their husbands and do not have the same desire for emotional intimacy as others. The question remains, then, if these wives would feel the same no matter who they were married to? Or would they feel more connected to, and show more concern for, their partner if he was not addicted to work? We only know that spouses are likely to experience these things when they are married to people who are addicted to work, but we cannot say for certain that the reason they have distanced themselves emotionally is because the person they are married to lives in his or her own "world of work".

A third study shows that spouses of workaholics have an experience of carrying the whole responsibility for raising the children and managing the housekeeping. This often makes them angry, and as a result they complain a lot (Robinson, 2001, p. 129). One can imagine how, in the beginning, it feels only natural that the person who spends the most time at home is the one who takes care of the housekeeping. But it will naturally become a burden as the family grows, and he or she has been left alone with all the chores for a long period of time.

Characteristics of the partner of workaholic

Researchers have discovered that people who are severely addicted to their work often find partners who are not addicted to work (Robinson, 1998). Based on case studies and interviews, they have developed a portrait of the partners (*ibid.*). Based on Robinson's work, I describe below which feelings and experiences partners and spouses of workaholics have in common. They often:

- feel neglected, kept outside, unloved, and unappreciated because of the workaholic's physical and emotional distance;
- experience that they are left alone with the emotional responsibility for the marriage and as a parent. This leads to a feeling of loneliness in the marriage;
- feel that they are not being prioritized high enough by the workaholic, because spending time with the family is dictated by his or her job;
- see themselves as extensions of the workaholic—who is the centre of attention;
- have a sense of being controlled and manipulated and sometimes hurried by the workaholic, who sets the pace;
- are attention-seeking in relation to the workaholic in order to reach him or her;
- see the relationship as something serious with almost no time for fun;
- have a sense of guilt because they want more from the relationship;
- have low self esteem, because they feel unable to live up to their partner, whom they have often put on a pedestal;
- question their own gratitude and sanity when faced with the accolades bestowed on their workaholic partner.

There are, thus, a number of feeling and experiences that are characteristic of the workaholic's partner. The central feelings are the feeling of inferiority and the sense of being lonely within the relationship. It is not necessarily because the person addicted to work is *intentionally* excluding the partner that these feeling occur. The feelings of the partner may have something to do with the positive and admirable qualities that the workaholic possesses. Characteristic of the workaholic is, among other things, their self-discipline and their stamina. Even though they are tired and have been working for hours, they are likely to continue working. In addition, many workaholics are focused on results and performance, which means that some of them will climb the career ladder quickly. If the partner puts him or herself up against these qualities and results, he or she may often feel inferior because they cannot do the same.

Consequences for the children

As we have seen in a previous section, a severe addiction to work is often followed by a number of negative consequences for the workaholic's partner and children. But how does the behaviour of the parents affect the children in the long run? A study was conducted to discover if children whose fathers or mothers are (or had been) addicted to work would develop problems as adults that other children did not have (Carroll & Robinson, 2000). The study compared three groups of men and women in their twenties. In one group they all had a parent who was a workaholic; in the second group they all had a parent who was an alcoholic; and in the third group they all had parents who were not addicted to anything. The study showed that the adult children of workaholics had a much higher degree of depression and parentification than the other two groups. Parentification means, as I explained earlier, that the child behaves as a mother or a father towards other members of the family. The child puts aside his or her own need for attention, comfort, and guidance in order to respond to the emotional needs of the parent(s) or other family members (as described on pp. 51–52) (*ibid.*).

Similar studies have shown that adult children of workaholics show compulsive tendencies to a greater extend than others (e.g., Robinson & Kelly, 1998). They are likely to do things without any realistic purpose, such as, for instance, performing rituals. In addition, they also find it hard to find any internal motivation and are rather motivated by rewards from the surroundings such as admiration and wages. These adult children are also more prone to anxiety, and show a higher degree of external locus of control than children whose parents are not addicted to work. External locus of control is, you will remember, when you experience having no influence on your own life but feel that what happens to you is caused by external circumstances.

These studies show that it can have serious consequences for you if one of your parents has been addicted to work. Having grown up with a workaholic might lead to your having mental/

psychological problems as an adult. You actually have a greater risk of developing certain problems if you had a parent who was a workaholic than do children of alcoholics, even though these children's childhoods were characterized by anxiety and betrayal (Carroll & Robinson, 2000). The risk of developing depression, for instance, is higher if your parent was a workaholic than if your parent had been an alcoholic (*ibid.*).

How the workaholic perceives the family

In addition to studying how the partner of the workaholic perceives the marriage, there have also been studies as to how the workaholics perceive their families. A study in which 107 American and Canadian workaholics participated indicates that an addiction to work is related to dysfunction in the workaholic's family (Robinson, 2001). The addiction was measured on the basis of the test on p. 43. Those who had the highest score (67–100), and who were consequently categorized as "highly workaholic", had a markedly different experience of their families in comparison with the non-addicts and those with only milder degrees of addiction. In comparison with the other two groups, the severely workaholic experienced their families as less able to solve problems and communicate with each other. They also felt that in their families they were less emotionally involved with each other, and that family members expressed their emotions less frequently. They also felt that people in their families did not pay adequate attention to each other's activities and worries. The study shows that the more addicted you are, the more dysfunctional you think your family is.

Marital problems and divorce

Neal is thirty-nine years old and married for the third time. For several years he has been working in a law firm. He says himself that he has been "really far out", and that for many years he has done nothing but work. "I have always been very committed to my work, and never thought about whether it was too much. When my second marriage failed, I realized that I might not always be easy to live with. In a way I had been cheating on my wife, because my work had taken up all my time, and was always the most important thing to me." Neal explains how he did not respect his first or his second wife when she asked him to put aside his work. He does now. It is important to him that his marriage is a success this time, and he does not want to make the same mistakes as before. "I realize now that my work habits affected my family. I often had to check my e-mails in the evening, and if it was bad news I came back into the living-room in a bad mood." Neal still works a lot, and his wife has to remind him to take time off. He emphasizes, however, that things are much better than they were before.

The workaholic's relationships are often characterized by arguments and problems (Robinson, Carroll, & Flowers, 2001). Sometimes, the partner does not believe that the nights in the office are spent on work, but suspects the workaholic of having an affair. One in three men who work long hours have been accused of cheating (Weeks, 1995).

Studies show that workaholics spend an excessive amount of time on work compared with time spent on their marriage; at the same time, they also have higher expectations as to what a happy marriage is (Robinson, 1998). Different studies have also shown that the more "obsessed" you are with your work, the less happy you will be with your marriage (e.g., Gabbard & Menninger, 1989). A partner addicted to work is described as one of the four main reasons for divorce (Robinson, Carroll, & Flowers, 2001). It is not the actual job, or the fact that the workaholic wants a career, which destroys the private life; it is rather the negative feelings that these priorities might create in partner that are destructive (Bartolome & Evans, 1980).

It is impossible to say if the cause of any divorce is the result of a person being addicted to work. It is, therefore, also impossible to say if the conflicts in a marriage arise from one person being addicted to work, or if, on the other hand, the person is addicted to work because of the unhappy marriage. Both explanations could be true. It is not difficult to imagine how the husband or wife of a workaholic often feels alone and abandoned when the partner puts his or her job before anything else. We are also all of us able to relate to how it feels to argue with one's partner. It is an unpleasant situation that we try to avoid. A valid reason for being away from home is the call of duty, and this could be the solution some people choose to avoid conflicts at home.

As we have seen in this section, it might have several negative consequences when work takes control of a person. It might have unfortunate consequences for oneself, but it might also affect one's partner and children. One of the biggest problems for the family is the physical and mental absence of the person who is addicted to work. This might lead to some family members experiencing a number of negative emotions, which they direct towards themselves or the person addicted to work. The family might quickly be caught up in "vicious circles" in which conflicts are either escalated or maintained. As I have described in this chapter, several studies point to the fact that there are often different kinds of problems in the families in which one adult is addicted to work. We know, therefore, that marital and family-related problems are related to this phenomenon. In some cases, however, it is unclear whether the addiction is the direct cause of the problems within the family. In order to shed any new light on this, it is important that further studies are conducted on this topic.

The workplace

Consequences for the workplace

One would think that the more committed a person is to his job and the more time he spends on it, the better it is for the company. This, however, is not always the case. A few of the researchers who see an addiction to work as something positive claim that these individuals are an asset to the company (Korn, Pratt, & Lambrou, 1987). They perceive the workaholics as hard-working and conscientious, and, consequently, as highly valued employees whom every employer would want working for them. The majority of scientists working in this field, however, disagree with this (for example, Robinson, 1998; Spence & Robbins, 1992). They point to the fact that it can lead to problems as well as financial losses for the company if they employ workaholics.

Those individuals who have lost control of their work are prone to push themselves and to continue working no matter how long they have already been working and how tired they are. They have the ability to overstep the boundaries as to how much they can perform. This, however, often means that they become less efficient. One might even say that their strength is also their weakness. Employers naturally see it as a good quality that employees make an effort and work for many hours every week. However, if you push yourself too hard over a long period of time you become inefficient. If you are rested and full of energy, you will be more productive at work; if, on the other hand, you are tired and overworked, your efficiency will decrease and you will not get the most out of your time. If, over a long period of time, you work too much and do not allow yourself to "recharge your batteries", your brain and body will not have time to recover. You will become exhausted and lose track of things and consequently you will make more mistakes. It is commonly known that we get our best ideas when we stop working and start to relax. To get away from work and do something completely different for a couple of hours may get your creativity flowing. For example, spending some time outside may lead you to see the solution to a problem that may have bothered you for a long time.

Workaholics are, as I have mentioned, often perfectionists (Spence & Robbins, 1992). In many ways it can be an advantage to be a perfectionist; it might, however, also mean that the person is slow and inefficient because he is afraid of making mistakes, and could therefore find it difficult to finish a job. Workaholics are, as described earlier, reluctant to delegate tasks to colleagues because it gives them a greater sense of control to be in charge of as many areas of the work process as possible. In addition, it may also give them greater knowledge and thereby the feeling of being important to the company if they are involved in a large part of the tasks that have to be carried out.

Stress

As I described earlier, addiction to work is related to stress. This means that the majority of people who are workaholics are also stressed. The level of stress will usually vary over a period of time, just as it will be different from one person to the other how they react to it. The problems that might develop in a workplace which employs workaholics are closely related to stress. It could be physical and mental reactions to stress, such as those described earlier in this chapter, which impair the employee's ability to perform. In addition to this, the reactions might also have a negative impact on the mental work environment. Symptoms of stress might be difficulty with remembering and concentrating, which will affect one's ability to solve problems and complete tasks. Furthermore, fatigue and indecisiveness could also impair one's work performances. Bursts of rage, irritability, and a poor sense of humour are also characteristics of stress. If a person displays any of these symptoms, it could affect clients and colleagues, and thus impact the psychological work environment in a negative way. The many physical symptoms related to stress will usually also impair one's ability to work: these include dizziness, nausea, headaches, and muscle and abdominal pains, and are but a few of the physical reactions to stress, which means that a person is unable to function properly. Stress could also, as mentioned earlier, lead to depression and serious physical illnesses such as heart disease. Stress is, therefore, a problem that leads to a waste of resources and actual losses for the company.

Employing people who push themselves to work all the time will often create different kinds of problems. One should, therefore, weigh the quality of the work that the employee performs above the number of hours he spends at the job. The manager of a Scandinavian company is not impressed with people who stay at the office all night. She sees it as a sign that they are unable to manage their time and are rather unstructured. If we are to be efficient employees and at the same time achieve a good balance between work and our private life, we and our employers both need to focus on quality instead of quantity. The individual employee could remind him or herself to work more efficiently instead of working longer by repeating the phrase, "Work smarter—not harder".

CHAPTER SIX

What can we do if our work takes control of us?

"Work is the refuge of people who have nothing better to do"

(Oscar Wilde, quoted in Robinson, 1998a, p. 232)

What do we do if our jobs start to take control of our lives? Or if we notice that our partner, our sister, or a colleague has no time for anything but work? We usually think that the problem will solve itself. It will become less busy at work soon, and then we will have more time to do other things. But, if we are suffering from work addiction, the problem is not how much work we have to do, but our work patterns, as they exist over a long period of time.

If you are addicted to your work, you cannot count on your workload suddenly getting smaller unless you make a conscious effort towards it. However, there are several things you can do if your work has taken control of you, or if you want to prevent it. You can also make a difference to those people who are too involved in their work, but who may not be aware of the consequences of this. It is very important to do something if you are concerned about another person's way of living and working. Most people are afraid of meddling in other people's lives, but it is better to show concern, and thereby care, instead of passively looking on while the work habits of another person result in the breaking up of his family, for example.

The professionals, who work with different types of addiction essentially agree that the addict has to be 100% abstinent (Steffen, 1993). The individual has become addicted because he was not able to control how much of a given substance to take. He should, therefore, abstain from the "drug" from now on, so as not to lose control once more. This, of course, is not a desirable solution when it comes to work. And, in terms of economics, this is indefensible. As a result, no single solution can be put forward as to how the workaholic prevents his work from taking control of him again.

In this chapter we look at the things we can do ourselves to achieve a balance between our private and our working lives. In addition, we discuss how the family, colleagues, and the management at the workplace can help the person who has lost control of his or her work habits. The last part of the chapter deals with what can generally be done to prevent a rise in the number of workaholics in the future.

What can the workaholic do himself?

If work takes up too much of your time and you want to achieve a better balance in your life, you can follow some general advice. The most important thing to do is to take responsibility for your own situation; you should not expect things to change by themselves, or hope that others can or will create the changes you wish for. It is no use expecting your family to set limits for your work life if you have not been able to do so yourself. However, people around you, at work, your friends, and your family can provide valuable support, and it is a good idea to encourage them to do so.

This section is based on the experiences of three former workaholics, who share with us how they achieved a better balance in their lives. These men, who are mentioned in Chapters Four and Five, are Jonathan Lazear, David Adams, and Steve (Lazear, 2001; Jürgensen, 2003; Rasmussen, 2004a). Jonathan Lazear, who owns a publishing house, as mentioned earlier, wrote the book *The Man Who Mistook His Job for A Life*, which deals with his own life as a workaholic. David Adams was the head of an advertising agency, but fell ill due to exhaustion caused by his job, and was appointed another job in the company. Steve was working at a company that expected its employees to dedicate their lives to the job. He eventually resigned. For several years, these three men were caught in a work trap, but now they have changed their lives and once again have families, friends, and free time on their hands.

The first steps

Do nothing

If you suddenly realize that your work is controlling you, the first thing to do is to do nothing (Lazear, 2001)! Workaholics are in the habit of rushing along, solving any problems they might face right away. The secret, now, is to do the opposite and not do anything at first. Nobody is able to change their life in a short while; in this case, you are not dealing with a task that has be finished by a certain date. If you try to solve the problem quickly, you have not changed your behaviour and you have not taken the necessary time to get in contact with your own self. Your thoughts and emotions can guide you and help you to a better balance. It is, therefore, necessary for you to discover what you are feeling.

Be alone

It takes time and peace of mind to find out why you are cluttering up your life with work (Rasmussen, 2004a,b). The best thing to do is to organize some time off for you to be by yourself and do nothing. This will give you an opportunity to reflect on how you live your life, and how you want to live it in the future. It may help you to think about what makes you happy, and about the things that are most important to you. You can also try imagining being seventy-five years old and looking back at your life. What was missing? What would you have liked to do differently? By contemplating these questions you may discover your basic values and, then, let them be guidelines for the direction in which you want to go.

Ask for support

If you are unsure as to whether your work habits are causing problems in your family, it is a good idea to talk with the members of your family. They might have a completely different view of the situation than you think. You could also talk to your friends and colleagues in order to get a more balanced image of how other people view your involvement in your work.

It is difficult to change your life without getting support. Lazear (2001) thinks that it is impossible to get rid of the work addiction unless you get help. Many people who are controlled by their jobs are used to solving any problems themselves and find it difficult to ask for help. However, it is a good idea to get your family or colleagues to support you. Your colleagues can remind you that it is time to go home and your family can make sure that you do not work when you are at home. Having people around you who support you and whom you are willing to listen to, can be of great importance. This way you will not face the challenges alone.

Be patient

The next step is to accept the fact that it takes time to change one's habits (*ibid.*). It took a long time to acquire these inappropriate work patterns and it will probably take some time to get rid of them. This is why patience is important. If you are a Type A person, characterized by always feeling pressed for time, it will be a great challenge for you to stay patient.

Free time

Slow down

Staying in touch with your feelings and needs takes peace and quiet. If you lead a very active, and maybe even hectic, life, peacefulness, introspection, and a slow pace are necessary as a counterbalance. This counterbalance can help you ward off stress. It is healthy to sometimes do nothing and be bored, because boredom can set off your creativity and lead you to create and develop new things. To relax, immerse yourself in a hobby, go outside, or explore other sides of yourself than those used in your job; these can all be welcome "breathing holes" that give you renewed energy. The problem with work addiction is that the many hours spent at work prevent you from experiencing and enjoying these activities/ places in which you can breathe more freely. In time, these possibilities might disappear completely from your mind, and you can imagine doing nothing else but work.

Take time off

One of the most important things to do is to clear your diary. You need to prioritize time off so that the workday does not continue indefinitely. It may be helpful to fix a time in your diary at which you go home. And then keep it, no matter what happens. Excuses will probably surface as to why it is necessary that you stay on a bit longer than initially planned. It is important to be consistent, and keep to the appointment. You may also decide to take the weekends off. In the beginning, it may be too much for you to take both days off if you are used to working all through the weekend. It would, therefore, be more realistic if you start by taking one day off. When you are "off" it is important that people are not constantly calling you with work-related issues that you have to deal with. It is also tempting to check your e-mail when you are at home, but it can easily take up more time than you expect it to. Besides, you have to deal with the content once you have opened the e-mail. This will often lead your thoughts to be preoccupied with work, so that you are not relaxing mentally. It is much better to commit yourself not to going online in the evenings and on your days off. This will prevent you from becoming a slave to the technology, and being controlled by it, instead of you controlling it.

Get a hobby

One way of forcing yourself away from the job is by getting a hobby. That is what David Adams recommends. He changed his own life by buying a boat and taking up fishing. He thinks it is important for the workaholic to get a life outside the job, something that forces him away from work, physically as well as mentally (Jürgensen, 2003). If you cannot think of anything that interests you, you may think of what you took pleasure in as a child or teenager.

You may also want to resume a hobby that you have now replaced by work.

See other people besides your colleagues

It is a good idea to see other people besides your colleagues. This will force you to think and talk of other things than your work. The free time you get by cutting down on your working hours may very well be spent on any friends you may have, outside the workplace. You could also seek out a new social network, for instance, in a sports club.

Feel your body

Your body gives you information about how you are doing and of any imbalances in your system. If you are always working and focused on the job you do not have the energy to notice your body and focus on what is happening within it. Many workaholics have only a vague sense of how they are feeling. They are used to subjecting their bodies and psyches to an enormous amount of pressure, and as a consequence they can endure a lot. For this reason, they are inclined to ignore the body's warning signals. One way of getting in touch with your body and your emotions is sitting in a chair for 10–15 minutes every day. You should close your eyes and direct your attention towards your body. This is also an exercise in relaxation and in "doing nothing".

At work

Prioritize your time

If you want to find the time to do other things than work, you need to be more efficient during the working hours, so that you do not need to be working all day and all night. This does not mean that you have to work faster; it means that you have to prioritize your tasks. Several former workaholics say that it is important to get a better overview of one's work, and to generate more time, by prioritizing the different tasks at hand (Jürgensen, 2003; Lazear, 2001). How many of the things you do are important, and how many unimportant? Try to get rid of the things that are unimportant.

Plan your breaks

Appoint time for breaks in your diary. It is important that you do not squeeze too much into one day. This helps you to prevent your day from becoming hectic. At the same time, you make sure that you have enough time to do your tasks to everybody's satisfaction. Some tasks may take up more time than planned, and it is important that you allow for this in the day's schedule. By aiming at having enough time for everything you have to do, you provide yourself with the best conditions for avoiding stress. If you feel that you do not have enough time, you become stressed. In the past couple of years, we have become accustomed to doing several things at once—as I mentioned earlier. The result, however, is that we become less efficient because we have to concentrate on several different things when multi-tasking. If we strive to do only one thing at a time, we become more efficient. In addition, we may also avoid accidents caused by our mind being unable to keep up with us because of the fast pace.

Talk to your manager

If you have too much to do over a long period of time, it is important that you talk to your manager about it. If you do not, the situation may never change. The responsibility lies with your superiors if you are too busy. It is not only your own responsibility, but also the responsibility of the manager if his employees are stressed or burnt out. You could tell him that you find it difficult to leave off work and that it is affecting your private life. You might also say that to continue being an efficient employee you need the manager to help you set limits for your working hours, so that the job does not take up all your time. This is a positive approach that shows that as an employee you want to do your best at the job, while at the same time being a "whole" person who has time for other things besides work. With this as a starting point, you and the manager might come up with a solution as to what would be the best thing to do for you.

A good conscience

If you work in a place where several of your colleagues work too much and are stressed, it is important that you do not let yourself get carried along. You should not feel guilty about going home before your colleagues, despite any slighting remarks. Instead, you should insist on going home.

Break the taboo

It is not easy for us to admit, in the workplace, that our work has taken control of us. We usually boast about how involved we are in our work and how many hours we work. To be able to combat work addiction we have to acknowledge that it exists and that it can be a problem if a person is controlled by his work. If work addiction remains a taboo, the addiction will develop and be made worse in those who are already affected by it. If you acknowledge that you are controlled by your work, it may lead some of your colleagues to discover that they are controlled by their work, too. Maybe you need to be the first one to break the taboo in order to create some new standards for what you can talk about at the workplace. Besides, some patterns are easier to break if you are not alone in doing it. If several people in a group of co-workers are all, to some degree, addicted to work, they can support each other in going home at the end of the workday instead of creating a culture in which the standard is that everyone stays late.

Get a new job

If it turns out that you are working in a company that promotes work addiction, the only solution may be to quit your job. That is what Steve did, and he recommends others in a similar situation to do the same (Rasmussen, 2004a). If changing the state of things is not possible, then a new job may be the best solution if you want to take care of yourself. However, there is always the risk of the addiction staying with you if you are still inclined to get caught up in the job. But fighting the work addiction becomes much easier if the environment does not prevent you from making the necessary changes. If you are predisposed for work addiction, and if you have been caught up in the work trap before, it is very important that you take notice of the company culture in your new place of work. You can ask to speak to one of the employees with whom you will be working, and ask them the questions you may not want to ask at the interview. This is one way to learn about the actual work hours, about the work patterns of the other employees, and what work standards apply.

Finally

Allow mistakes

Take small steps. You should not expect great changes immediately, but you should strive to make small changes. It is important to allow yourself to make some mistakes and do the opposite of what you had decided to do (Lazear, 2001, Robinson, 1998a). If you decide to take the whole weekend off, but still find yourself sitting in front of the computer on Saturday afternoon, it does not mean that you are a total failure and will never succeed in changing your work patterns. Many workaholics are perfectionists and will demand a lot of themselves in relation to dealing with this new challenge. The more of a perfectionist you are, the harder it will be for you to be satisfied with your own efforts. It is important to accept that you are doing the best you can, instead of focusing on the mistakes you may make.

Consult a professional

If you suffer from a severe case of work addiction, and have had no luck changing your life, one option might be to consult a professional (Robinson, 1998a). With the help of a psychologist you can examine what mechanisms are at the root of your behaviour. In addition, the therapist can help you change your work patterns if you are motivated to do so. If you seek the help of a professional, you have to be motivated to change certain aspects of your life. If you do it merely to please your family, and do not wish for the changes yourself, it is a waste of money.

What can we do to avoid stress?

Stress is one of the problems connected with work addiction. Workaholics often overwork themselves, physically as well as mentally, by being, in some way or another, preoccupied with their job twenty-four hours a day. If your work takes up most of your time, you are at risk of developing stress. The risk is high with workaholics, because recreational activities and relaxation are not a part of your life and therefore cannot counterbalance the strain of working all the time. As a workaholic you have the added risk of being stressed because of the Type A personality described earlier, which is characteristic of the workaholic and makes them more vulnerable to stress and other health-related problems. Stress can also have great emotional and social costs, and it is a good idea to know how to prevent these. In this section we will look at what you can do yourself to combat stress.

Identify symptoms and stressors

As we discussed in the section on stress in Chapter Five, it is a big help if one knows the symptoms. If you do, you will quickly realize that you are stressed and you will be able to do something about it. A lot of the symptoms of stress are physical, and because of this you might think that their cause is physical, but this might not be the case. In addition to knowing the general danger signals, it is a good idea to get to know your own symptoms. By doing this you will quickly be able to decide if the psychological, behavioural, and physical changes are caused by stress.

The next step is to find out what has provoked the stress: in other words, what changes have occurred around you? The change does not have to be in your surroundings. It may be a change in your way of thinking about different issues that has caused the symptoms of stress you are experiencing. If this is the case, the challenge may be for you to start thinking more positively and be more optimistic in your attitude. Perfectionism and fixed ideas about how things *ought to be* can also stress you. It would, therefore, be for the best if you could change these modes of thinking. If the cause of your stress is external, you could try to change it. You might, for example, be doing several things at the same time, such as rebuilding your house, studying for a higher qualification, and taking care of your aged parent, and you may feel that you are unable to manage all these things. In a situation like this, you should change your expectations to match your own abilities. The key word here is prioritizing, and you will have to choose to focus on the things that are most important to you. You should be realistic in your expectations of your own abilities. It may also be the case that the stressors are at work. Are certain circumstances in the job provoking the stress symptoms? You should try and change these. It may turn out that certain aspects of the job will not change or cannot be changed. In a situation like that, it may be necessary for you to find another job.

Recharge your batteries

You can do several things if you are stressed or want to prevent yourself from becoming stressed (Dipboye, Smith, & Howell, 1994). One of the most important things to do is to get enough sleep. While you are asleep your body recuperates, and sleeping will also provide you with the energy you need to deal with the physical and mental challenges of everyday life. Stress can lead to insomnia and disturb your sleep pattern; it is, therefore, vital that you get enough sleep if you are feeling stressed.

Another way of dealing with stress is by relaxing and "recharging your batteries". If you are already feeling stressed it may be difficult to relax, but it *is* possible to force your mind not to think of the job by doing something completely different. One way of "recharging" is to spend time on a hobby, or with your family and friends when you are not at work. Playing a game with the children on a Saturday afternoon, or going to a café with a friend, are both recreational activities that force you away from work. At the same time, these activities strengthen some of the other roles you play in life, such as, for instance, mother or friend. This way, you avoid identifying yourself solely by the role you play at work. Recreational activities also create a balance between the different areas in your life and prevent it from becoming one-sided and only about work. By doing something other than work, and by seeing other people besides your colleagues, you also strengthen your relationships with others. Having a social network means that you can have different kinds of support. Social support, such as talks, encouragement, practical help, and the like, is one of the factors that can help prevent or relieve stress. This is why having friends who will support you is such a benefit. In the life of the workaholic there is not much space left for recreational activities, because work takes up most of the person's time. Because the workaholic spends less time on recreational activities, he is more at risk of developing stress.

Exercise and meditation

Another way of preventing and relieving stress is by exercising (Dipboye, Smith, & Howell, 1994). When you are physically active, the excess adrenalin you produce in a stressful situation is carried to your muscles. In addition, endorphins, which work as pain-killers and elevate your mood, are released. As a result you feel relaxed and comfortable after the exercise, instead of stressed. In addition to exercise, meditation, yoga, and relaxation exercises are efficient and popular ways of reducing stress. The problem when using sports or the techniques of the East as a way to combat stress is that the warnings from the body, such as symptoms of stress, are toned down. The signals indicating that you should change some aspects of your life are removed. This can make it difficult to find and remove the things that cause the stress.

Exercise, yoga, mediation, and relaxation exercises that can help you combat stress could also be misused. This happens when these methods are used to push the body even further in order to be able to work more. Several workaholics have said that they sometimes force themselves to go for a run, because it gives them extra energy so that they can work even more. Some addicts, it would seem, view sports as a tool to optimize their work effort. Physical activity, which can be a source of great physical and mental pleasure, should not be reduced to a necessary evil that helps you maintain an increasing pressure at work.

Stress is related to work addiction, and the heavy workload that an individual will subject himself to might be what causes it. It will, thus, make a positive difference if you can get rid of the work addiction, as this will greatly reduce your risk of stress, health problems, and the feeling of being burnt-out. It is, however, practical to combat both the addiction and the stress at the same time, as this will help you achieve a better balance in your life. If you make a whole-hearted effort in both areas, you have a better chance of achieving the changes you desire.

What can the family do?

It is hard on the family if a person is too involved in his work. For one thing, he may be absent, both physically and mentally, most of the time. He may also value his work more than his family, which leads his partner and children to feel that they are not important to him. A family member should remember that the only way the workaholic can change his ways is if he wants to do it himself. His partner and his children cannot change his habits for him, even if they want to. The family can, however, influence whether a person who is predisposed to this kind of addiction will develop it, and might thus be the deciding factor that prevents a person from being controlled by his work. In addition, the family can do several things in order to prevent the work addiction from developing further if it is already present.

Plan activities

A family's standards with regard to spending time together may help to prevent or stop someone's disappearance into his own world of work. If you do not already have certain traditions and unwritten rules about spending time together, it is a good idea to introduce them. Your family may decide to spend Saturday evenings together in the future. Or father and son might plan fishing trips, just as mother and son could introduce a weekly trip to the public swimming pools. Even though it could seem inflexible, it might be necessary to schedule such activities, making it less likely that they will get cancelled because of things you may find more important. Having arrangements like these is better than having made no promises at all to each other. If your partner and your children insist that these commitments be kept, and, for instance, do not accept you cancelling a holiday, it might prevent you from becoming controlled by your work. These commitments might also be necessary in order to get your everyday lives to work properly. You could, for instance, introduce a rule saying that everyone has dinner together at seven, every night. This might not suit the person who is used to being absorbed by work, but it may help to prevent the work from taking up more and more of that person's time. Commitments and planned activities with family (or friends) might prevent the person from spending all his time at work.

Recreational activities, such as a hobby or sports, are a good contrast to being absorbed in your work, because your thoughts are forced away from the job. After spending time doing such activities, you will have renewed energy and, one hopes, you will have experienced the joy that comes from being creative or from exercising.

Share chores

For a family to function, a number of practical chores have to be taken care of; for example, cleaning and cooking. To avoid work taking up all of your or your partner's time, it is a good idea to share these chores. You can, for instance, take turns at cooking or picking up the children. In this way, one person is not responsible for the household chores alone while the other one is spending all his or her time at work.

Tell him that he works too much

Addiction will sneak up on you and develop gradually. It is, therefore, of vital importance that the family of a potential workaholic expresses concern about him getting too involved in his work. There will be times when he works more than usual, without him noticing it. In situations like this, it is important that those close to him point his attention to it. They have to remind him to take time off, and to set limits for his working hours. It is important that they emphasize how much they want the person back. If they do not, he is at risk of becoming controlled by his work.

Tell him that he is missed

If a family member is addicted to work, it is important not to be too focused on the changes the person has to make. If the workaholic is constantly pressured to stop working too much, he could get so used to hearing the same message that it will, eventually, have no effect on him. Being angry and frustrated that your parent or partner is not spending as much time at home as you would like him to might lead you to make demands and utter admonitions. This, however, will lead the workaholic to think that you are nagging him. Hence, he might react by defending himself, instead of listening to what you are actually saying; that he is missed by his family. You could, then, enter a vicious circle in which conflicts escalate instead of the family spending more time together. The best way to motivate the person who is too consumed by work to stay at home more is not to criticize his behaviour. It is better to tell him that he is missed. Such a positive declaration of love will not seem like an attack, but rather like an honest announcement of how the family is feeling.

Let him take responsibility

As described in Chapter Four, the family will sometimes cover for the workaholic by making excuses on his behalf as to why he does not participate in family or social events. It is, however, important that he is forced to assume responsibility for his own actions, as he should not be allowed to escape the guilty conscience that is the result if you let other people down. Experiencing such guilt might lead the addict to discover the consequences of valuing his work over his family.

Appreciate him for who he is

If you feel valuable as a person, you are less inclined to have to perform well all the time. It is, therefore, important that the family appreciates the workaholic for *who* he is, and not for *what* he does. The human qualities and not the performance should be appreciated. Instead of taking him for granted, it is important to express how much you appreciate him. By doing this, he may become less inclined to seek recognition through his work.

The best thing would be for the workaholic himself to recognize that his work habits are causing problems, and for him to want to change them. In a situation like that, his partner and children may become his allies. In this way, they are more likely to be of help to him, as they are not working against him by nagging and criticizing him.

What can we do at the workplace?

We spend a lot of time at our place of work every day, and, as a consequence, we influence the place and the people we work with, just as they influence us. If the management and staff wish to prevent their employees from being so caught up in their work that it starts to affect their health, families, and even the company itself, they have to take certain precautions. The circumstances that affect the employees are the company culture, the rules at the workplace, and the management's attitudes and values. In this section, we discuss what management and employees can do at the workplace to prevent and combat work addiction and stress.

Talk about company culture and work patterns

In every workplace a company culture exists. It is determined by the traditions and standards that apply in a particular place. We do not usually question the company culture in our place of work, because we are a part of it. The ruling standards are invisible; they are not spoken and they have not been written down. As a result it becomes somewhat intangible and diffuse having to relate to one's own company culture. Nevertheless, the culture and values that are related to our workplace have an influence on our lives when we are at work. Our behaviour, not to mention our development and how comfortable we are in being there, is closely linked to the company culture. As a consequence, it has a great impact on whether or not the workplace promotes or inhibits work addiction. Employees, as well as management, are all responsible for the culture they create.

Considering that the company culture is both invisible and diffuse, it may be helpful for employees and management alike to talk about what standards and traditions actually apply. By doing this, our behaviour is made visible and we may become conscious of appropriate and inappropriate patterns that we did not see before. Is it all right to phone a colleague on his days off to ask about work-related issues, and thus invade his privacy? Do we have an unwritten rule that no one leaves before 6 p.m.? Will a person be subjected to slighting remarks if he leaves earlier? The next step would then be to discuss why things are as they are, and find out if there are things we would like to change. In a discussion like this, a culture that encourages work addiction would be made visible. In addition, conditions that may promote stress are also identified, and might be changed now that we can see them.

One way of revealing any potential problems is to start talking about them. Many people who feel stressed, or believe that work has taken control of them, are reluctant to share their feelings with colleagues or their managers. Despite the fact that stress is all over the media these days, many people are afraid to admit that they are feeling stressed. They see stress as a sign of weakness and evidence of their inability to do their jobs. In times of cutbacks, this reluctance might be caused by a fear of being fired. It could also stem from the fact that we do not have a tradition of opening up to each other in our place of work. One way of changing this pattern is to break the taboo and start talking about these things. Management as well as employees can take the initial steps towards a discussion of work habits. One starting point could be a talk held at the workplace that would provide opportunity for a discussion of these issues. A company could, for example, take up these issues in its works committee or safety committee as a way of bettering the mental work environment.

Several employees in a large IT company outside Copenhagen had started to feel that their work was taking up almost all of their time. They managed their own working hours, and nobody asked them to work overtime, so they had no actual problem to take to the management. Still the dissatisfaction grew. These feelings were shared only with the colleagues whom they trusted the most. It was not something that was openly discussed in the company—only face to face. For this reason, a works committee took the initiative to call a meeting, after work hours, focusing on work addiction. The meeting consisted, among other things, of a presentation on work addiction, which led to a discussion of this subject, and thereby made it acceptable to talk about the employees' personal experiences.

Make mutual agreements

In many jobs, the employee controls his own working hours, and essentially functions as his own manager. As many people are conscientious in relation to their jobs, this can easily lead the individual to work overtime every day. A culture in which everyone works long hours can encourage work addiction in those individuals who are predisposed to it. It is difficult for the individual to

break a norm, and most people will probably adapt to the unspo-
ken rules, instead of fighting them. It might, therefore, be a good
idea to talk about what norms apply, and to discuss if some of them
need to be changed. Talks such as these will often show that a large
number of people are dissatisfied with these standards, but are
convinced that everyone else is comfortable with the existing
circumstances. A joint dialogue may lead the employees to decide
which values and norms should be predominant in the company
culture. If several people in the group feel that work is taking up
too much of their time, it may be beneficial for everyone if they
agree to support each other in going home earlier. The advantage
of this approach is a greater chance that each employee will come
to work the next day feeling rested and refreshed, thus being a
more efficient employee. In addition, it allows the individual
employee to achieve a better balance between different activities in
his life, so that it does not damage his health or his family.

What can management do?

Appreciate the balance between work life and private life

One of the challenges for the management is to create values for the
company that result in a comfortable, engaging, and innovative
environment. This may be done with the knowledge that financial
results are connected to a series of values that are deeply rooted in
the company. In relation to this, it is of great importance what attitude management has to the balance between work life and private
life. If the management rewards the people who work excessively,
it may create a company culture that encourages work addiction.
However, seeing it as an asset that employees are "whole", and
have lives outside the job, will prevent them from burying themselves in work. If excessive work is not appreciated, the employee
will not feel as motivated to do so. Many people, however, are motivated by the recognition they get from colleagues or clients, and,
then, the attitude of management is not enough to stop them from
becoming too involved in their work—even though it still holds a
central position.

George A. Schaefer, the managing director of Caterpillar (the
producer of, among other things, contracting and mining equip-
ment, diesel and natural gas machines) is one of the managers who

feel that it is important for the employees to create a balance between their work lives and their private lives (Robinson, 1998). According to him, life has four sides. One side represents our work life, the second our internal life, the third our family life, and the fourth our leisure-time life. For Schaefer, all four sides have to be lived if we are to be healthy, happy, and productive people. He does not want to employ workaholics. He does not feel that they are efficient employees in the long run, because they usually do not want to delegate their tasks and are not good at prioritizing.

Set limits for working hours

Today, when work and leisure-time merge, in many jobs one of the biggest challenges is to set boundaries so that work does not consume all your time. If this is not done, the endless work will eventually lead to work addiction and stress. Most of us find it difficult to set these boundaries, and it becomes necessary for the management to step in. It is vital that management is made aware of the benefits of cutting down the work hours, instead of increasing them. One benefit is that the company avoids having to pay the expenses connected with employees who have to take leave because of stress or because they feel burnt out. In addition, an employee who has achieved a balance between work and private life is much more efficient than an employee who exerts himself by working all the time. Thus, the management's motivation for setting limits for the working hours can be both moral and financial.

One way of setting limits for the work hours is by having distinct rules for counterbalancing overtime, and by having a manager who notices if his employees take time off or not. The management may also say directly to the employee that they do not want him to stay in the office late in the evening. If the management makes the employees understand that it is better to have a good rest in the evenings, so that they can come to work the next day feeling rested and refreshed, it may also prevent a tendency towards work addiction. In addition, the management may advise the employees not to take their work home in the evenings, or on their days off (Jespersen, 2004; Tylor, 1999). In Sweden, a number of companies are worried about their employees. One company, for instance, orders its employees home after the normal work hours, and asks them to show up the next day rested and refreshed with new ideas. You do not have new ideas if you are worn out, they say (Stenstrup, 1998).

Be a good role model

One of the ways, in which a manager can show that he prefers the employees to have a life outside work is by setting the standard through being a good example. The manager acts as a role model to the employees, and has to demonstrate the behaviour he wants to dominate the workplace.

The manager often works more hours than the employees. This is possible without the person being a workaholic, because the addiction is not solely defined by the amount of hours spent at work. The important thing is for the manager to show that he has a life outside the company, and that he does not encourage a standard which demands that he is in the office every night, sending e-mails and calling his employees on their days off.

Insist that your employees have breaks

As the head of a company, you can insist that your employees have their breaks, so that they unwind a couple of times each day, instead of straining themselves by working non-stop (Tylor, 1999). Many people do not feel that they have time for breaks, and they eat in front of the computer in order to make the most of the time. Apart from it not being very appropriate that employees cannot unwind, it will also harm the social environment at the workplace if people do not meet and chat. Thus, there are several reasons why insisting on breaks is a good idea. It may even be a good idea to make it part of the company culture for everyone to meet and have a break together. You could, for instance, all gather for a cup of coffee and a snack at 10 a.m. every day. By making it a joint understanding, it becomes part of the culture, instead of something each individual employee is responsible for. To strengthen the feeling of community and promote good health, while at the same time making sure that the employees have a 10–15 minutes break, you could introduce a joint exercise lesson. Almost 1500 employees in Denmark are already part of the popular initiative; "exercise by mail", which was introduced by the county of Frederiksborg and

The Danish Association of Company Sports (TV2, 2004). The participants receive a description of an exercise in their e-mail box every day. These exercises can also be performed in the company of one's colleagues, and it thus becomes a tradition to meet for a break in the work every day.

Avoid unrealistic deadlines

Deadlines are necessary in many jobs, and are often a source of stress and of employees having to work overtime. The best thing to do, although it is often difficult, is to plan the work so that you do not have to spend long hours of extra time at work. Sometimes this is not possible, as you have several deadlines within a certain period of time, and it is unrealistic that you can finish within normal working hours. Too many, or unrealistic, deadlines can lead some people to work too much all the time. However, the manager could help by organizing the work so that there are no impossible deadlines hanging over any one employee. In situations in which the deadline cannot be changed, and in which work has piled up, one way to help may be to delegate some of the work to others, so that the workload of each individual employee is lessened. Deadlines are one of the areas the manager needs to keep an eye on, in order to prevent the company from becoming a place that encourages work addiction. In some places, the employees are given contrary information. It may, for instance, be emphasized that deadlines have to be met, while at the same time employees are told that they have to take care of themselves. The latter is hard to do if certain projects or tasks have to be done by a certain, unrealistic deadline or within a very short time-frame. It is a good idea for the management to enter into a dialogue with the employees when the work is to be organized. In this way, the employees can influence when the job is to be finished, so that stress and overtime may be eliminated or at least limited.

Choose staff benefits carefully

Staff benefits are valued by employees. It lies in the term itself that they are something positive. They may be financial advantages, material goods, or certain conditions in the workplace that make the work day more fun, or more comfortable, physically as well as mentally. In the past couple of years, new types of staff benefits have started to appear. Companies have taken various steps in their efforts to make the life of the individual employee easier and thereby increase his efficiency and performance. In this way, staff benefits are beneficial to employee and employer alike. Some companies have, for instance, introduced free dinners for those working overtime, a workstation at home, including access to the internet, free mobile phone, massage and physiotherapy at a discount, just to mention a few.

It was the IT business that, some years back, was the first to introduce untraditional benefits. The media told of hard-working IT employees who had practically moved into their places of work. Pizza was delivered to the door, they had a bed in the office, free cola in the refrigerator, and entertaining games in the hallway. All these things made the workplace a homelike and comfortable environment. It was an evident merging of the professional and private lives. The young computer chaps were always working, so why should they waste time going home to sleep? They had nobody waiting for them at home, and their friends were at the workplace. Their work became their lives. It is easy to imagine how much the employees enjoyed these benefits. Everything they needed was within reach, and they did not need to go home. The environment was homelike in several ways, and it motivated the employees to spend more time at work than they would have done under normal circumstances. The management was probably very satisfied with the extra hours the employees put in as a result of these initiatives. The tempting offers at the workplace, which benefit most people, can, for some employees, be pitfalls. If you are prone to devoting your life to the company, these types of benefits can promote a lifestyle in which you live solely for your job, and become addicted to work. This is why management have to be aware of any individuals who show a predisposition for becoming over-involved in their work, and they must consider carefully what kinds of benefits they will introduce.

One example of staff benefits that can help strengthen a balanced life is if the company has a link with a fitness centre. Many companies have arrangements that allow the employees to exercise free, or at a reduced price. Such a benefit will not only be a benefit to the individual employee's health, it will probably also be beneficial to the company in the long run, as it will reduce the absences due to illness. At the same time, this kind of staff benefit will help to prevent and combat work addiction, because it motivates the staff to get away from the workplace and to take time off and exercise.

Certain conditions in a workplace may thus prevent, provoke, or maintain an addiction to work. If the management of a company wants to prevent employees from developing this kind of addiction, they should consider if certain conditions encourage the staff to work excessively. For this reason, staff benefits should be chosen with care, and in an ongoing dialogue with the employees as to what disadvantages these might entail. Cases will inevitably occur in which a single staff benefit will further work addiction in one employee, while at the same time being nothing but an advantage for another. In other instances, certain benefits will cause the work hours to get out of control in one company, whereas the same benefit, when introduced in another company, will not affect the amount of hours worked at all. When benefits are introduced it is important to take into account how the majority of employees act, and advantages have to be set against any disadvantages.

Help each individual employee

If an employee has too many tasks, and finds it difficult to delegate some of them, it may be necessary for the manager to step in and assume responsibility by actually taking some tasks away from the employee. Then it will not be the heavy workload that maintains the work addiction. It may also be necessary to make clear which areas are the responsibility of each individual employee. As an employee, it is important to know where your responsibilities lie, so that you do not worry about things that are not your concern. In some cases, it may be hard to define these responsibilities, especially in a project-based organization. In those cases it is important that time is spent clarifying these individual responsibilities, as they may be vital to the well-being of the staff. If an employee cannot limit his involvement in the job, and is overworking himself with too many tasks, it may be necessary for the manager to help him. Together they may figure out what will be the best thing to do under the circumstances. In some cases, psychological counselling or therapy may be the best solution.

Managers are not able to see and sense everything that is going on in a company. It is, therefore, important to emphasize that even though the manager is ultimately responsible for providing help, the employee is equally responsible for speaking up and asking for help. In order for the employee to be willing to speak up, and even to show his vulnerability to the management, the company culture has to be open and safe. Creating such a culture will prevent employees from being guarded and hiding their problems instead of drawing attention to them and thereby solving them.

How do we avoid stress in the workplace?

In addition to the human inconveniences connected with stress, it may also result in great financial costs for the company and for society as a whole. Stress has wide-reaching consequences and should be taken seriously by the individual as well as by managers and politicians alike. If we are to combat work addiction, we need to change our attitudes. As long as prestige entails being busy and working a lot, it will be difficult to change people's lifestyles and their work habits. In addition to this, we have to start talking about stress and not be afraid to admit when we are not feeling well. We also have to discuss the conditions at work that can lead to stress, get involved in coming up with solutions, and be willing to change the way we act as well as our attitudes. Furthermore, we should not be afraid of addressing a colleague who shows signs of stress.

Many people are reluctant to act when they see that another person is having a difficult time. The excuse we make for not acting is that we do not want to interfere with other people's lives. If we disclaim any responsibility for the people around us, and only show indifference, it may make matters even worse. It is, therefore, better to talk *with* him than to talk *about* him. If we address him in a respectful way, and express concern, not criticism, in relation to the person's situation, there is a good chance that our approach will be received positively. In this way we may help to prevent a person from developing stress and the health problems connected to it.

In order to reduce the amount of absence due to illness caused by stress, we need to prevent stress instead of acting only when the damage is done. This could be achieved by focusing on the mental work environment. The knowledge that we already have concerning stress can be used to prevent new cases. We know, for example, that social support at work reduces stress (Netterstrøm, 2002). Therefore, we have to limit the amount of "alone-work" which is a result of more and more people working at home. Company managers should also take note of the employees' well-being. They should be made responsible when conditions in the workplace promote stress. This is far from the case today. Certain cases, for instance, of sexual harassment and particularly bullying, are extremely hard to prove and can cause stress and lead to people being absent because of illness (Jelstrup & Loldrup, 2002).

In connection with the large amount of attention given to stress these days, individual stress management has become a central issue. Today, courses on stress management are on offer everywhere, and current books take up the issue. It is, of course, helpful to learn how to deal with your own stress. The disadvantage of concentrating on stress management, however, is the risk that stress becomes the exclusive responsibility of the individual, instead of *also* being the responsibility of the company management. It may be very beneficial to work with stress prevention on an organizational level, and thereby improve the mental work environment in general. Thus, you will be able to take action, not just at the level of the individual, but also on a group and an organizational level. In doing this, it would be useful to turn to psychologists or consultants who have experience with organizational initiatives and prevention of stress.

Management's task is to provide the best possible settings for work, so that stress and other health problems are prevented. It is, however, important that we, as employees, take responsibility for our own situation and recognize the amount of influence we have on the workplace. Through our way of acting, we all influence each other in the workplace; therefore, we all share in the responsibility of how the place works. If we do not recognize this influence and responsibility, but instead put it all on the shoulders of management, we come to see ourselves as victims of the circumstances, instead of active participants. Any organization is the product of its constituents. Therefore, any good management needs a good company.

What can we do as a society?

In this chapter we have been discussing what the workaholic can do himself, and what his family and workplace can do to prevent and combat workaholism and stress. As described in Chapter Four, the overall environment that is our culture and society can provide a setting that either prevents or encourages us to work too much. Thus, we have to be critical of certain aspects of society if we are to prevent a development that has our work controlling us, instead of it being the other way around. In addition, politicians and unions have to use their influence to secure the best possible conditions for each individual to achieve a work–life balance.

An important tool, in relation to this, is education and information (Christensen, 1999). The public has to be informed of the consequences of overworking oneself for a long period of time. In addition, the Minister for Health and Minister of Employment could initiate a campaign that encourages people to adhere to a week of thirty-seven working hours, and to take holidays and days off. Today, we have a right to a number of holidays, but we are not obliged to take them. The campaign should thus inform of the risks connected with not prioritizing a balanced life and free time. As mentioned earlier, it can harm your relationship, your children, your health, and your mental state if you do nothing but work. A campaign such as the one mentioned should include scary examples of the consequences it can have if work takes control. This method has been used in other campaigns; for instance, in describing how much of a difference speed makes in traffic accidents. The best approach would, of course, be to motivate employees and managers to achieve a balance between the different areas of their lives. If this approach is not successful, it may become necessary to legislate on the subject in order actively to try to prevent work addiction. It could, for example, be made compulsory that you take your holidays. You could also limit the workload of each individual by taking in more people when a job has a workload which is equal to two people working normal hours. Some people will argue that, as a community, we cannot afford to work less if we are to retain jobs and be competitive at an international level. The real question, however, is if we can afford to have people working so much that they become stressed, ill, divorced, or neglect their children, or, in the worst cases, die prematurely (*ibid.*).

Another way of combating work addiction on a general level is by involving an organization such as The Work Foundation. This is a not-for-profit organization that exists to campaign for good work, and could help with advice and guidance on making the conditions in a place of work sound in relation to preventing and combating work addiction. This is an important consideration if Western companies are to avoid seeing instances of a cause of death that is related to over-exertion caused by excessive work. Most cases of this to date occur in Japan, as mentioned before, where, in 2006, 155 workers died as a result of overwork (*karoshi*). Sixty per cent of *karoshi* cases have done at least 100 hours of overtime a month (Lewis, 2007). Cases like this may already have occurred in the UK without us being aware of the cause. A greater knowledge of work addiction will offer us an opportunity of preventing this type of death in the future.

Had this been a different problem, involving the same serious consequences, politicians would probably already have been appointing committees and initiating campaigns. Why has this not happened yet? In the Western world we have, as mentioned earlier, a tradition for appreciating hard work and rewarding those who do something out of the ordinary. Those who do nothing but work are often lionized in the media and viewed as role models. Maybe politicians refrain from putting limits on our working hours for fear that the wheels of society will then come to a standstill, and the public develop a taste for the free time. For the politicians to be convinced that this is an area that needs prioritizing, we have to attach figures to the problem. We have to find out how many people are addicted to their work, and to what degree they are addicted. It would then be possible to conduct a study of how great a cost to society this phenomenon is. Faced with such a study, politicians should see the need to make a general effort to prevent the number of workaholics from rising in the future.

CHAPTER SEVEN

Will work control us in the future?

Several different conditions of today's society indicate that work will be given an even higher priority in the future. The out-phasing of family life, the possibilities of information technology, the high demands in education, and the individualized demands on performance all point in the same direction: work will come to take up more time and space in our lives in the coming years. In earlier times, work was merely a means of survival, but several things indicate that work will come to be an independent goal of life (Lindhardt & Urhskov, 1997). As things are today, there is a great risk that work will come to take up more time and occupy more space in our minds in the future. Because of technological developments, we are now able to work independently of fixed time and space, and the job has long since invaded our private sphere. The pace is faster than ever before and we are optimizing everything. In the name of efficiency we have dropped our lunch-breaks, so that we now eat in the car, in front of the computer, or at so-called lunch meetings. Our internet connections become faster and faster and our mobile phones can do virtually everything these days. According to occupational health psychologist Einar Baldurs-son, all of these circumstances make our work limitless (Sonne,

2003). This means that work takes up more and more space in our lives. Based on these circumstances, several experts predict that in the future we will see an increasing number of people who become addicted to work.

Jonathan Lazear, who used to let his work dominate his life is worried that we are in the process of making a new generation of workaholics of our children (Lazear, 2001). He points to the fact that many parents often boast about how many hours their children spend on homework and how well they do at school. This emphasis on hard work and performance motivates the children to work even harder. The child gets positive attention when it is persistent and achieves good results. This may form the basis of a life centred on being something by virtue of one's performances. As an adult, it will be natural for the person to seek this form of recognition in a job, and he or she is then at risk of becoming overly focused on work.

Occupational health psychologist Einar Baldursson also predicts that we will see more people losing control of their work in the future (Rasmussen, 2004b). He argues, among other things, that our society is promoting over-involvement in the job. He sees the problem as occurring as early as in primary school, in which the children are trained in this through project-based work. Project-based work requires a great commitment and an ongoing work effort until the product is finished. You are in charge of your own work hours and this may present a challenge, as many people experience being pressed for time when it comes to project-based work. People working on a project will often not take any time off, and if they have breaks the project is probably on their mind, so that they are never completely "off". The number of project-based assignments has exploded in primary schools in recent years, and, according to Einar Baldursson, project-based work is a form of narcotic over-involvement that we as a society reward. The argument for teaching children and adolescents this method of work is that project-based work is the work form of the future. Today, we see job advertisements for project-based positions and temporary positions with the sole purpose of solving a single task.

The US magazine *Fortune* predicted, as early as 1994, that changes in society will mean that permanent jobs as we know them today will completely disappear in the future (Lindhardt &

Urhskov, 1997). According to the magazine, the "job" was created 200 years ago, because the industrialized society needed it. Now that the world has changed, we no longer need this artificial invention. Concurrently with increasing privatization and outsourcing, we have begun to see the need for companies having a variety of different tasks solved. This tendency may lead to an increase in part-time and other temporary work situations, which will eventually replace permanent jobs. A number of people are, as mentioned, already employed in project-based positions. When the work that companies need to have done is constantly changing, the inflexibility of the permanent job is inappropriate. Permanent jobs will therefore die out because they are too rigid and inflexible. *Fortune* recommends that we do away with permanent jobs and redesign organizations so that they will make the most of the adaptability of the workforce. There will still be plenty of work to be done, but it will not be done within the present framework called "job". In the future, thus, there will be fewer employees and more entrepreneurs and self-employed people. This will increase the risk of more people becoming addicted to work. The situation one faces when being self-employed is, especially in the first few years, rather insecure, and demands a great effort if one wants to establish oneself and survive in spite of the competition. This may lead people to become too involved in their work, and they may risk becoming addicted.

Today, our work situations are not as stable as they were in earlier times when people used to stay in the same job all their life (Mogensen & Larsen, 2003). The "lifespan" of companies are generally shorter than they used to be, and we cannot expect to work for the same company for many years. Because of the expansion of the Internet, the world has become one big market-place, where only the most skilful and those who are willing to change survive. This puts new demands on the employees, who are expected, above everything else, to be flexible. In order to keep one's job today, or to get a new one, you have to constantly upgrade your knowledge and develop new qualifications. Experience and education no longer guarantee that companies will need you. You are being assessed by what you create, and you are only as good as your last project. If you are unable to keep up and to perform, you risk losing your job. This puts constant pressure on the individual employee and may lead him or her to work too much in order to keep his or her job.

In the report *10 tendenser mod år 2010* (10 tendencies towards 2010), from the Institut for Fremtidsforskning (Copenhagen Institute for Futures Studies), 20–30% of all work today is characterized as UFO work (Mogensen & Larsen, 2003). UFO work means udefinerbare, flydende opgaver (indefinable, fluid tasks) and these tasks are characterized by being stimulating, highly responsible, and self-fulfilling. UFO work is project- and knowledge-developing work centred on different tasks that need solving. This kind of work is attractive today, even though it is unstable and puts great demands on the individual to develop and use his or her whole being in the work. These changeable and demanding jobs will be a reward to those who are comfortable in such positions, while others will become stressed and see the personal and professional challenges as a burden. No matter what you think of this kind of work, it demands that you are 100% committed to it. The more involved you get in this kind of job, the greater the chance that you will achieve good results. The downside is the increased risk that the work will come to control you, instead of you controlling the work.

Not all experts think that the current development will lead us to become completely dominated by work in the coming years. Futurologist Morten Grønborg (2003) predicts that a large number of people will react against the invasion of work into our private sphere, and will try once again to separate work and leisure-time. Some people will have a need to be *off* instead of *on*—mentally as well as technologically. They will demand their right to quietness and to taking time off. Another group will continue along the same track and only make small changes in their lives. They will continue to use technology uncritically, maybe even to the point that they will begin to suffer from a technological "Always online syndrome", which some physicians predict will become the new national scourge.

Today, the lives of thousands of people are characterized by business and a fast pace. Why do we rush along and constantly keep busy? Maybe we are afraid of the silence and emptiness that would ensue if we took some time off. Loneliness, when only your own thoughts and feelings keep you company, may seem scary to some people. The busier you are, and the more hectic your life is, the greater is the risk of losing control and contact with oneself and the people closest to you. We risk that time for reflection will disappear if we prioritize activity and work above everything else. Technology has helped to set the fast pace in several areas of life, but we are able to choose when and how much we want to use these technological aids. No one is forcing us to send 100 text messages a day or to have our computer turned on all the time. If we want to prevent ourselves from becoming the slaves of our own development we need to decide first how we want to live our lives, and second, what things bring us quality of life and joy. Some people have already begun to get rid of the needless and the things that make them stressed. This tendency is called simple living. We have to decide if we want to work seventy hours a week, and risk our bodies and families saying, "no more". For a large number of people it will be a challenge to reduce their ambitions and give high priority to balance instead of running faster and faster and aiming higher and higher.

There are several currents in society today and in our way of living our lives that indicate that work will come to take up much more space in our minds and take up more of our time in the future. The technological development has meant that many manual labour jobs have become obsolete. As a result, more people today are employed as so-called knowledge workers; these jobs make work limitless, as they do not tie employees to time and place. You are free to work whenever you choose, but sometimes creative ideas come when you are off work, and then suddenly you are "at work" at an inconvenient time. Many of us have probably experienced standing in the supermarket and suddenly having a great idea for work, or losing concentration in the middle of a conversation with your partner because you suddenly thought of something you had to remember in connection with work. If this happens a lot, work may begin to dominate your life and take control of it at the cost of your private life. Concurrently with many of us being employed in so-called "knowledge appointments", we have gained more responsibility. We have become our own bosses, among other things, because we now control our own career and our work hours. This has given the individual employee more freedom, but it has also led to the responsibility and worries that used to be the concern of the manager now becoming our own. As a consequence, it may be difficult, if not impossible, to put one's job aside when one is off work. In addition, there is always something that one can improve, go through one more time, or new knowledge one can acquire, when one is at home. Many people describe how they always feel that they are left behind, because the amount of knowledge available via the Internet makes it virtually impossible to be updated with the latest information. If we give in to our own high demands and expectations as to how much we ought to know and how much we ought to work, it may lead to work taking control of us. If you want to avoid losing control of your work habits and risk the consequences of this, it is important to be aware of the set of values you live by and to listen to how other people experience your commitment to work.

If we want to prevent and limit the number of people who become too involved in their work, we must each of us take action when we come across such individuals. Many of the people who have become controlled by their work do not realize it themselves, or they deny it to themselves and the people close to them. Their lifestyle has often characterized them for several years. The involvement in the job has probably increased gradually over the years without the person noticing it. Unhealthy work patterns have become normal for this person, and he does not question his own way of living. It is, therefore, very important that family, friends, and colleagues make him aware that his life is out of balance and point to the obsession with work that he might display. Whether the workaholic will change his work habits and his life in general depends on his being able to see the advantages of doing so. People close to him might try to encourage him, but real changes require that he is motivated to make them.

If we want to prevent more and more people becoming controlled by their work in the future, it would be best if efforts were made in several areas. If the individual, the family, the workplace, and the people responsible for making the laws of society all get actively involved in the discussion of work and its place in our life, and of the consequences an over-involvement in work may have, we have a greater chance of preventing work from taking control of people, leading to addiction.

REFERENCES

Axelrod, S. D. (1999). *Work and the Evolving Self. Theoretical and Clinical Considerations.* Hillsdale, NJ: Analytic Press.

Baldursson, E. (2002). Dum af stress. *Prosa, 5:* 6–7.

Bartolome, F. & Evans, P. A. L. (1980). Must success cost so much? *Harvard Business Review, 58:* 137–148.

Beck, U. (2002). *Fagre nye arbejdsverden.* Copenhagen: Hans Reitzels.

Bendtsen, N. (1985). *Homo Faber. Om arbejdets historie.* Forlaget Modtryk.

Berlingske Tidende (2003a). *Det store eksperiment.* 16 November.

Berlingske Tidende (2003b). *Arbejdet forstyrrer vores privatliv.* 16 November.

BibleGateway.com (English Standard Version).

Bonebright, C. A., Clay, D. L., & Ankermann, R. D. (2000). The relationship of workaholism with work–life conflict, life satisfaction, and purpose in life. *Journal of Counseling Psychology, 47:* 469–477.

Bonke, J. (2003). *Tid og velfærd.* Socialforskningsinstituttet. Nearly 3000 participants have been interviewed and have—like their partner—kept a detailed diary of how they spent every hour of the day.

Burke, R. J. (2000). Workaholism and divorce. *Psychological Reports, 86:* 219–220.

Burke, R. J. (2001). Predictors of workaholism components and behaviors. *International Journal of Stress Management, 8:* 113–127.

Carroll, J. J., & Robinson, B. E. (2000). Depression and parentification among adults as related to parental workaholism and alcoholism. *The Family Journal. Counseling and Therapy for Couples and Families, 8*: 360–367.

Chamberlin, C. (2001). Workaholism, health, and self-acceptance. *Dissertation Abstracts International, 62*: 1332-A.

Christensen, S. (1999). Arbejdsnarkomani. *Politiken*, 25 July.

Clark, L. A., Livesley, W. J., Schroeder, M. L., & Irish, S. L. (1996). Convergence of two systems for assessing specific traits of personality disorder. *Psychological Assessment, 8*: 294–303.

Covey, S. R. (1999). *The Seven Habits of Highly Effective People. Restoring the Character Ethic*. London: Simon & Schuster.

Csikszentmihalyi, M. (1991). *Flow. The Psychology of Optimal Experience.* New York: HarperCollins.

Dipboye, R. L., Smith, C. S., & Howell, W. C. (1994). *Understanding Industrial and Organizational Psychology. An Integrated Approach.* Forth Worth, TX: Harcourt Brace.

Danish Radio Documentry (2002). *Obsessed with work.* 27 February.

Danish Radio News (2004). TV news. 9 May.

Faber, P. (2004). *Fyns Amts Avis*, 4 August.

Fassel, D. (1992). *Working Ourselves to Death.* San Francisco, CA: HarperCollins.

Friström, L. N. (2003). *Arbejdsjunkie. Om arbejdsnarkomani og behovet for balance.* Gads.

Fyns Amts Avis (2004). 4 August.

Fyns Stifttidende, 1 August.

Gabbard, G. O., & Menninger, R. W. (1989). The psychology of postponement in the medical marriage. *Journal of the American Medical Association, 261*: 2378–2381.

Giddens, A. (1991). *Modernity and Self-Identity. Self and Society in the Late Modern Age.* Cambridge: Polity Press.

Graversgaard, J. (1994). *Udbrændthed. Bryd den onde cirkel.* Frydenlund.

Grønborg, M. (2003). OFF. *Medlemsrapport: 10 tendenser mod 2010, 4*: 22–23.

Grunnet, K. (1989). *Stress, job, livsstil.* Dansk Arbejdsgiverforening.

Hauschlidt, S. S. (2004). *Et liv uden stress.* Kassander.

Hundevadt, K. (2003). *Kanten af kaos.* Jyllands-Postens Bøger.

Husén, M. (1984). *Arbejde og identitet.* Nyt Nordisk Arnold Busck.

Institute of Work Environment (2000). *Arbejdstid—arbejdsmiljø i Danmark. 2000.*

Ishiyama, F. I. & Katayama, A. (1994). Overwork and career-centered self-validation among the Japanese: psychological issues and counselling implications. *International Journal for the Advancement of Counselling, 17*: 167–182.

Jelstrup, A-G., & Loldrup, H-O. (2002). *De onde og de dumme. En bog om destruktiv ledelse*. Frydenlund.

Jensen, M. (2001). *Tendenser i tiden. En sociologisk analyse af mobilitet, miljø og moderne mennesker*. Samfundslitteratur.

Jespersen, P. M. (2004). Vores arbejdsiver er sygelig. *Politiken*, 11 December.

Jørgensen, A. S. (2002). Familieliv giver stress. *DJØF-bladet*, 4: 4–5.

Jürgensen, J. (2003). Bekendelser fra en arbejdsnarkoman. *Markedsføring*, 8: 10–12.

Killinger, B. (1991). *Workaholics. The Respectable Addicts*. Firefly Books.

Korn, E. R., Pratt, G. J. & Lambrou, P. T. (1987). *Hyper-Performance: The A.I.M. Strategy for Releasing your Business Potential*. New York: John Wiley.

Lazear, J. (2001). *The Man Who Mistook his Job for a Life. A Chronic Over-Achiever Finds the Way Home*. New York: Crown Publishers.

Lewis, L. (2007). Downside of Japanese recovery is death by overwork. *The Times*, 18 May. Accessed at: www. business.timesonline.co.uk/ tol/business/economics/article1805819.ece

Lindhardt, J. & Urhskov, A. (1997). *Fra Adam til robot. Arbejdet historisk og aktuelt*. Gyldendal.

Machlowitz, M. (1980). *Workaholics. Living with Them, Working with Them*. Reading, MA: Addison-Wesley.

Maslach, C., Jackson, S. E., & Leiter, M. P. (1996). *Maslach Burnout Inventory Manual* (3rd edn). Palo Alto, CA: Consulting Psychologists Press.

McMillan, L. H. W., O'Driscoll, M. P., Marsh, N. V. & Brady, E. C. (2001). Understanding workaholism: Data synthesis, theoretical critique, and future design strategies. *International Journal of Stress Management, 8*: 69–91.

Milsted, T. (1999). *Stress. Sådan tackles stress*. Børsen.

Mogensen, K. Æ., & Larsen, G. (2003). No comfort zones. *Medlemsrapport: 10 tendenser mod 2010*, 5: 18–21.

Netterstrøm, B. (2002). *Stress på arbejdspladsen. Årsager, forebyggelse og håndtering*. Hans Reitzels.

Netterstrøm, B., Laursen, P., & Paludan, L. S. (1996). *Arbejdsmiljøundersøgelse af lokomotivpersonalet ved DSB*. [A Work Environment Research of the Train Personnel Employed by the Danish State] Copenhagen: Arbejdsmiljøfondet.

134   REFERENCES

New York Times (2003). 6 July.

Nielsen, T. (1997). Tre slags arbejdsnarkomaner. *Psykologi Nyt*, 11: 28–29.

Nielsen, T. (1999). *Psykiske egenskaber. Om karaktertræk, evner og psykiske lidelser.* Dansk Psykologisk.

Oates, W. E. (1971). *Confessions of a Workaholic.* New York: World Publishing.

Perez-Prada, E. (1996). Personality at work. *Dissertation Abstracts International*, 57: 4763-B.

Pietropintro, A. (1986). The workaholic spouse. *Medical Aspects of Human Sexuality*, 20: 89–96.

Rajs, J., Perski, A., Blomqvist, V., Hammerstrom, E., & Hammerstrom, A. (2001). Arbejdsrelaterad stress bakom plötsliga dödsfall? Två unga svenskar drabbade av känt japanskt fenomen. *Ugeskrift for Læger*, 163: 1284–1288.

Rasmussen, P. (2004a) Unpublished interview with Steve. 5 July.

Rasmussen, P. (2004b). Unublished interview with Einar Baldursson. 18 July.

Robinson, B. E. (1989). *Work Addiction. Hidden Legacies of Adult Children.* Deefield Beach, FL: Health Communications.

Robinson, B. E. (1998a). *Chained to the Desk.* New York: New York University Press.

Robinson, B. E. (1998b). The workaholic family. A clinical perspective. *American Journal of Family Therapy*, 26: 65–77.

Robinson, B. E. (2001). Workaholism and family functioning: a profile of familial relationships, psychological outcomes, and research considerations. *Contemporary Family Therapy*, 23: 123–133.

Robinson, B. E., & Chase, N. D. (2001). *High-performing Families. Causes, Consequences, and Clinical Solutions.* American Counseling Association.

Robinson, B. E., & Kelly, L. (1998). Adult children of workaholics. Self-concept, anxiety, depression, and locus of control. *The American Journal of Family Therapy*, 26: 223–238.

Robinson, B. E., Carroll, J. J., & Flowers, C. (2001). Marital estrangement, positive affect, and locus of control among spouses of workaholics and spouses of nonworkaholics. A national study. *The American Journal of Family Therapy*, 29: 397–410.

Schaef, A. W., & Fassel, D. (1988). *The Addictive Organization.* New York: Harper & Row.

Scott, K. S., Moore, K. S., & Miceli, M. P. (1997). An exploration of the meaning and consequences of workaholism. *Human Relations, 50*: 287–313.

Sonar & Jyllands-Posten (1999). *Arbejde og uddannelse.* 13 September.

Sonne, C. (2003). Besat af dit arbejde?, *I Form,* 13: 60–65.

Sørensen, T. K. (2004). Stress og pres. *Jyllands-Posten,* 16 May.

Spence, J. T., & Robbins, A. S. (1992). Workaholism: definition, measurement, and preliminary results. *Journal of Personality Assessment, 58*: 160–178.

Spence, J. T., Helmreich, R. S., & Pred, R. L. (1987). Impatience versus achievement strivings in the Type A behaviour pattern: Differential effects on student's health and academic achievement. *Journal of Applied Psychology, 72*: 522–528.

Sprankle, J. T., & Ebel, H. (1987). *The Workaholic Syndrome.* New York: Walker.

Steffen, V. (1993). *Minnesotamodellen i Danmark.* SOCPOL.

Stenstrup, B. (1998). Når fast arbejde bliver et fyord. *Berlingske Tidende,* 13 December.

TV2 (2004). News. 9 November.

Tylor, K. (1999). Spinning wheels. *HR-Magazine, 44*: 34–42.

Weber, M. (1995). *Den protestantiske etik og kapitalismens ånd.* Nansensgade Antikvariat.

Weeks, D. (1995). Cooling off your office affair. *North West Airlines World Traveler Magazine,* June: 59–63.

Weinberg, R. B., & Mauksch, L. B. (1991). Examining family-of-origin influence in life at work. *Journal of Marital and Family Therapy, 17*: 233–242.

INDEX